Fram

Tony Harrison was born in Leeds in 1937. His volumes of poetry include *The Loiners* (winner of the Geoffrey Faber Memorial Prize), *Continuous*, *v.* (broadcast on Channel 4 in 1987, winning the Royal Television Society Award), *The Gaze of the Gorgon* (winner of the Whitbread Prize for Poetry) and *Laureate's Block*. Recognised as Britain's leading theatre and film poet, Tony Harrison has written extensively for the National Theatre, the New York Metropolitan Opera, the BBC, Channel 4, the RSC, and for unique ancient spaces in Greece, Austria and Japan. His film *Black Daisies for the Bride* won the Prix Italia in 1994; this and his volume of film/poems *The Shadow of Hiroshima and Other Film/Poems* and his feature film *Prometheus* are published by Faber and Faber. His most recent film/poem was *Crossings* (LWT), 2002. In 2007 his *Collected Film Poetry* was published by Faber and his *Collected Poems* by Penguin.

TONY HARRISON

Fram

faber and faber

First published in 2008
by Faber and Faber Limited
3 Queen Square, London WC1N 3AU

Typeset by Country Setting, Kingsdown, Kent CT14 8ES
Printed in England by CPI Bookmarque, Croydon, Surrey

A CIP record for this book
is available from the British Library

ISBN 0-978-571-24169-9

2 4 6 8 10 9 7 5 3 1

Acknowledgements

Grateful thanks are due as ever to Marion Holland for invaluable help with research, and to those actors who did a week's *Fram* workshop at the National Theatre Studio in 2006: David Bradley, Max Dowler, Michael Feast, Caroline Gruber, Tanya Moodie, Colin Stinton, Sian Thomas, Joseph Thompson and Peter Wight; and to Ann Morrish and Sian Thomas, who read extracts of *Fram* with me at the European Cultural Centre of Delphi, Greece, in 2006.

Tony Harrison
March 2008

Fram was first presented in the Olivier auditorium of the National Theatre, London, on 10 April 2008. The cast was as follows:

Gilbert Murray Jeff Rawle
Sybil Thorndike Sian Thomas
Fridtjof Nansen Jasper Britton
Hjalmar Johansen Mark Addy
Ballerina Viviana Durante
ARA Men
  Stuart Shaw Jim Creighton
  James Callaghan Steven Helliwell
  William H. Rutland Joseph Thompson
  Sheldon, ARA Chief (Moscow) Patrick Drury
Eglantyne Jebb Carolyn Pickles
Ruth Fry Clare Lawrence
Kurdish Poet Aykut Hilmi
Stowaways Ronald Chabvuka, Joel Davis,
  Verelle Roberts, Keanu Taylor

Directors Tony Harrison and Bob Crowley
Set Designer Bob Crowley
Costume Designer Fotini Dimou
Lighting Designer Mark Henderson
Music Richard Blackford
Video Designer Jon Driscoll
Choreographer Wayne McGregor
Sound Designer Gareth Fry
Production Manager Diane Willmott
Staff Director Max Key
Stage Manager Maggie Tully
Deputy Stage Manager Janice Heyes
Assistant Stage Managers Peter Gregory, Julia Wickham

Characters

Gilbert Murray

Sybil Thorndike

Fridtjof Nansen

Hjalmar Johansen

Ballerina

ARA Men

Sheldon

Eglantyne Jebb

Ruth Fry

Kurdish Poet

Stowaways

FRAM

Part One

*Westminster Abbey. The sound of late organ practice
echoes in the empty Abbey. Then the organist stops,
shuts off the organ, turns off the lights and we hear his
echoing footsteps reverberating in the Abbey and the
opening creak and echoing closing slam of a huge
wooden door.*

*Poets' Corner and across the way the memorial to
Gilbert Murray.*

*A cloud moves away from the full moon and its light
streams through the Rose Window, and sheds the image
of Aeschylus into the air like an Aurora. Then it falls on
the memorial plaque to Gilbert Murray.*

*Gilbert Murray emerges after fifty years beneath his
plaque.*

*He stands in the coloured light cast by the image of
Aeschylus.*

*He looks up at the Rose Window and addresses
Aeschylus.*

GILBERT MURRAY

Aeschylus? I don't believe it. You! You! it's you
in Westminster Abbey the moon is shining through.
My ecstatic ashes find themselves illuminated
by the spirit of the poet I'm so proud to have translated.
The light's like an Aurora and I rejoice, rejoice
that I was ever chosen to be your English voice.
Aeschylus! Your radiance is like the bright Aurora
described to me by Nansen, my friend, the explorer,
who's the protagonist I've chosen in the fifty years I've
    spent

composing my own drama beneath my monument.
Aeschylus! Aeschylus! O Aeschylus, I knew
the light that woke my spirit could only come from you.
So, greatest of tragedians, I beg you to assist
my humblest of efforts to become a dramatist.
With your inspiration I hope our play succeeds
in honouring Fridtjof Nansen and his heroic deeds,
from the Polar ice floes he sailed his ship the *Fram* in
to his noble role in saving millions from famine.

> *Gilbert Murray sees a fresh green laurel wreath
> laid on a plaque in the floor of Poets' Corner,
> though he doesn't see that it is laid on the memorial
> to T. S. Eliot.*

This drama I'm preparing 'll earn me a laurel wreath
like this one laid to honour the poet who lies beneath.

> *Takes wreath, then looks back at plaque.*

Oh no! Oh no! It beggars all belief.
T. S. Eliot! He's not worth one laurel leaf.
What a tasteless, not to say a crudely crass idea
to place Eliot in this spot when I'm not far from here.
What a dastardly, mean and spiteful trick to play
to put my cruellest critic just seventy feet away!

> *Gilbert Murray walks away from the T. S. Eliot
> memorial and tries on the wreath for size.*

This could be the laurel wreath I'll be allowed to wear
once I've shown the Muses my true poetic flair.
And once I've got the crown on I'll be finally allowed
to cross the floor to mingle with the Poets' Corner crowd.
Me in Poets' Corner! My deepest dream come true!
Provided they don't put me next to you-know-who!

> *Gilbert Murray begins to walk towards Poets' Corner
> to replace the laurel wreath, then decides to keep it*

and place it on his own memorial. He contemplates the wreath on his carved name.

I know! I need Sybil Thorndike, my Hecuba, Medea.
Her ashes, I believe, are also resting here.

Gilbert Murray begins to walk through the Abbey searching for Sybil Thorndike.

Sybil! It's Gilbert! I've been let out on parole.
I'm going to do a drama and want you to play a role.
Sybil! Sybil!

SYBIL THORNDIKE
Gilbert! No need to go so far.
I'm just round the corner from where your ashes are.
Right here next to Noël, who died in 1973.
I played Lady Gilpin in his *Hands Across the Sea*,
the same year I played Aphrodite and the Nurse
in your *Hippolytus*. I'm happiest with verse.
And your verse, whatever critics say, I find divine.
I went on playing your Medea till I was fifty-nine!

GILBERT MURRAY
I know that very well, that's why I wanted you.
There's a part in this drama I rather hope you'll do.

SYBIL THORNDIKE
What as?

GILBERT MURRAY
As yourself, dear Sybil.

SYBIL THORNDIKE
As myself, oh dear!
I get stage fright as myself.

GILBERT MURRAY
Please say that you'll appear.

SYBIL THORNDIKE

What's it about? Is it one of your translations?

GILBERT MURRAY

No, Sybil, an original, and my inspiration 's
Dr Fridtjof Nansen. I call my drama FRAM.

SYBIL THORNDIKE

Fram? Sounds like Beckett! Beckett SAM
not the Thomas à Becket of T. S. El—

GILBERT MURRAY

That name's taboo.

SYBIL THORNDIKE

Sorry, darling! Yes, he made cruel fun of you.

GILBERT MURRAY

T. S. Eliot! Who damned my versions of Greek plays,
saying they were ruined by my 'Swinburnian haze'.
'With no creative instinct he leaves Euripides quite dead'
is what you-know-who (that dreadful playwright!) said.
And would you believe it, the Abbey powers-that-be
have put his memorial only seventy feet from me!

SYBIL THORNDIKE

Surely, Gilbert Murray, this slightly petty streak
is scarcely compatible with chairs in ancient Greek!
Before I mentioned you-know-who and made you so upset
you said your play was called . . . what was it? I forget.

GILBERT MURRAY

FRAM ('FORWARD' in Norwegian), what Nansen called
   the craft
he had specially constructed with round hull fore and aft,
so that, when the pack-ice crushed it, it didn't crack, but
   rose
and stayed unshattered on top of the ice floes.
So with my modest talents as the would-be poet I am

6

that is my subject – Fridtjof Nansen and the *Fram*.
Fram, and famine, is the play I hope to write.

SYBIL THORNDIKE

Hope to write, Gilbert? When's it for?

GILBERT MURRAY

Tonight!

SYBIL THORNDIKE

Tonight? Tonight? But where's my part? We haven't time.

GILBERT MURRAY

But we're already talking in Gilbert Murray rhyme!
All you have to do is remember who you've been
and you'll be absolutely capable of playing any scene.

SYBIL THORNDIKE

Which theatre will have the honour of me playing me?

GILBERT MURRAY

The National Theatre, Sybil, on the South Bank, the 'NT'!
And, Sybil, you'll be thrilled to know that you will play
in the space named for your friend, Lord Olivier
(who resides near Poets' Corner, by the way).

SYBIL THORNDIKE
(*shouting*)

Larry?

GILBERT MURRAY

Not so loud! He'll hear you, and immediately start
demanding that he gets the drama's leading part.

SYBIL THORNDIKE

He'd be rather good as Nansen.

GILBERT MURRAY

No, Sybil, no,
it's only the originals I'm using in my show.

Nansen's Nansen. Gilbert Murray's me, and you, you're
    you.
Everything is real and everything is true.
I think it's time we quietly creep off to the NT
before all the ghosts of thespians start yearning to be free.

SYBIL THORNDIKE
Nansen was so handsome, I remember, like a Viking
when he came to London. To a lot of ladies' liking.
Will he be there?

GILBERT MURRAY
He will.

SYBIL THORNDIKE
                    Goody! But wish you'd said.
If I'd known I was meeting Nansen I'd've worn my red!

GILBERT MURRAY
You'll be fine just as you are!
                                Right! Across the river!
You'll appear after the Prologue I myself deliver.

*Gilbert Murray takes a marble mask from a poetic
memorial.*
    He takes Sybil Thorndike by the hand.
    *They hurry to the National Theatre. They go
through the foyers to the door into the Olivier stalls.
    They enter through the door to the Olivier stalls.*

SYBIL THORNDIKE
(*entering Olivier stalls through right aisle*)
Gilbert! This is so inspiring! The Olivier!
I can't wait to walk onto that stage and do your play.

GILBERT MURRAY
(*entering Olivier stalls through left aisle*)
Just imagine, Sybil, this space we see before us
was inspired by the theatre of ancient Epidaurus.

But the balcony's scarcely authentic ancient Greek.
Remember someone's up there, though, every time you
  speak.

SYBIL THORNDIKE

Gilbert you're addressing one who was renowned
throughout her lifetime for her clarity of sound.
Everything I utter will be crystal clear.
Even those in ten-quid seats have a right to hear.

Sybil Thorndike moves closer to the stage, then stops.

Gilbert, you resurrect me, give me no time to prepare,
let me come in the wrong frock and with frightful hair.
You should have given me time to choose another dress,
something less tomb-bound. Look, my hair's a total mess.

*Sybil Thorndike and Gilbert Murray go onto the
totally bare Olivier stage and savour its proportions.*

So you haven't got a text? And I see you haven't yet
gone to the trouble to think about a set!
I need costume and make-up, I don't want to disgrace
the memory of my noble friend whose spirit fills this space.
I need to change my costume. I need to do my face!

Sybil Thorndike exits.

GILBERT MURRAY

And while you are doing that I'm going to cover mine
to initiate our effort with one ancient tragic line.

*Gilbert Murray enters with the mask of Greek
Tragedy. He holds it before his face.*

Ουκ αν τις ειποι μαλλον η πεπονθαμεν.   (Eur. *Herc*, 916)

*Revealing himself, and placing mask downstage
centre.*

Not to cast aspersions on your state of education,

but is anyone out there in need of a translation?
Let me see a show of hands. O, I see, quite a lot.
No fellow classicists? Obviously not!
Ουκ αν τις ειποι μαλλον η πεπονθαμεν (*Herakles*),
one of the greatest tragedies of the great Euripides.
The messenger enters. His first words in Greek are these:
Ουκ αν τις ειποι μαλλον η πεπονθαμεν.
What he's saying 's that the horror that's occurred 's
too terrible for anyone to put into mere words.
And then from line nine-two-two to ten-fifteen
he lets us know in detail the horrors that he's seen.
Ninety-three lines in graphic, passionate succession
giving the unspeakable poetical expression.
Forgive the ancient Greek. I'm only showing off.

He bows.

Gilbert Murray, classicist, translator, prof.
As the ghost of Gilbert Murray I've not had to travel far,
just from Westminster Abbey where now my ashes are.
They've been there fifty years exactly. Hence this brief
    parole
and anniversary outing for my long-departed soul,
suddenly awakened by a streaming radiant light
that inspired me to rise and visit you tonight.
I'd hazard a surmise most of you are unaware
there's a stained-glass Aeschylus in the Abbey over there.
I was his translator. There's no poetic fire
blazes brighter in the firmament than his *Oresteia*.
His *Oresteia* was played here, and my question's why,
when my own was in existence, was the version by . . .
(permit me, I beg you, my peck of peevish pique)
a grubby Yorkshire poet with a bad degree in Greek!

Gilbert Murray composes himself.

I'm here as one who had the honour to know between
    the wars

one of the greatest heroes of the international cause,
my friend, Fridtjof Nansen, who died nine years before
our precious League of Nations broke up with the war.
Nansen was a hero who served the League of Nations
starting with his prisoner-of-war repatriations,
then giving the stateless person and the refugee
a means of crossing borders, an ID,
that allowed, for example, many a Russian émigré,
Stravinsky, Chagall, Pavlova, world-renowned today,
to use the special passport that bore his name,
the Nansen passport, to cross frontiers, and find fame.
Now Time's bestowed a Nansen passport on my ghost
to re-enter life and cross extinction's border post
to tell you I, like Nansen, a passionate believer
in the principles of peace we worked for in Geneva,
had to witness the League's failure, and, unlike Nansen,
   then
lived to hope for better from the newly named UN.
Nansen died. I lived, and to my profoundest shame
saw the atrocities enacted in humanity's soiled name.
To speak of the war's atrocities is an almost hopeless task
even for this open-eyed and eloquent Greek mask.
I happen to believe that the ancient tragic speech
is the highest form of eloquence a man can hope to
   reach.

*Sybil Thorndike in a dressing gown over a green dress
shouts from wings.*

SYBIL THORNDIKE

Gilbert!

GILBERT MURRAY

Sybil?

SYBIL THORNDIKE
Is it time for me yet?

GILBERT MURRAY

Not yet, no!
Your scene comes after Nansen's scenes in Arctic ice and
    snow.

SYBIL THORNDIKE

Scene? Scene! I can't believe you'd be so mean
to bring me back from oblivion to play one paltry scene!
How cruel to disturb a long-departed soul
only to offer her a less than leading role,
and make her wait while Nansen tries to reach the Pole.
Well, I hope his Arctic *scenes* take Dr Nansen ages.
It will give you time to write me several more pages.
I warn you if my part 's not a satisfactory size
I might have to steal the limelight and simply improvise.
And Gilbert, this costume, I fear that it won't do!
I never appear in costumes in either green or blue!
I can't go on, I warn you, dressed the way I am.
Find me another frock or you can fuck your *Fram*.

GILBERT MURRAY

Language, Sybil, language! I fear that you abuse
the purer vocabulary of my more genteel Muse.

SYBIL THORNDIKE

Well, Gilbert, I hope she won't prove so genteel
she won't do justice to the way that people feel.

GILBERT MURRAY

There are moments, I confess, when she rather shies away
from certain aspects of the subject that I've chosen for
    my play.
Though I admire Nansen with an almost schoolboy awe
I can't cope with the fact he's a fervent carnivore.
As a lifetime vegetarian I find that I can't bear
to describe what was for Nansen his daily Arctic fare.
The bear-brains breakfast fried in blubber of skinned seal
is not what I'd consider a tolerable meal.

And as a teetotaller too my non-imbibing Muse
is somewhat prim and squeamish about Johansen's 'booze'.
Nansen's companion. Johansen, who can only think
of surviving the Arctic to destroy himself with drink.
I don't want our audience out there to have to sit
listening to Johansen craving shots of *aquavit*.

And to be honest, Sybil, my Muse draws the line
at having crude four-letter words in anything of mine.

SYBIL THORNDIKE
Sorry!
      You and Nansen, such a diverse twain.
Strange that you were friends.

GILBERT MURRAY
            Allow me to explain.

Screen with UN emblem flown in.

I first met Fridtjof Nansen underneath this sign
representing, as it does, half his world and half mine.
That emblem up above me, he and I first met beneath –
the world from an odd angle enclosed with olive wreath.
The half I think as mine 's, of course, the wreath of
    peace,
representing what inspires me in the world of ancient
    Greece.
Nansen's half of the emblem is the skewed lopsided view
of the globe we're alarmed by because unaccustomed to.

SYBIL THORNDIKE
Why *is* the map lopsided and askew?

GILBERT MURRAY
It's the world as seen as if it's one united whole
but from the viewpoint of the nationless North Pole.
It amused Dr Nansen, the first man to have been
as near to the North Pole as 86 14,

that we first became acquainted underneath this sign
representing as it does half his world and half mine.

SYBIL THORNDIKE
Has Dr Fridtjof Nansen read anything by you?
If and when he sees his part will he know what to do?

GILBERT MURRAY
Dr Fridtjof Nansen is my most fervent fan!
Inordinately fond of poems that rhyme and scan!
Free verse appals him. He scorns the sort of Muse
that gives us rhymeless poetry like you-know-who's.
My verse, he assured me, was much to Nansen's liking
and him a man of action, an adventurer, a Viking!
Considered the most adventurous and glamorous man
    alive
when he almost reached the North Pole in 1895.
The complete man of action, a universal hero
who proved himself at temperatures of fifty below zero,
actually read and praised my verse translations.
He packed his head with poetry for Polar explorations.
You'd think a man of his kind, when he headed for the
    Pole,
would think about the body's needs and not about the
    soul,
but Nansen's shelves of poetry were packed inside his head
when only absolute necessities could be loaded on a sled.
Nansen's head 's replete with poems. I know none
    repleter.
He won't have any problems with Murray rhyme and
    metre.

SYBIL THORNDIKE
So while his many scenes show him expert in your verse,
if you can spare a moment, may we, *please*, rehearse?
And while Dr Nansen brings the Arctic into sight,
you, Gilbert Murray, have a lot of lines to write.

You're the last person needs reminding that in my long
   career
I have given my Clytemnestra, Hecuba, Medea.

*Sybil Thorndike drags off Gilbert Murray, who rushes
back to retrieve the tragic Greek mask.*
   *Enter Nansen. A lantern-slide screen flies in. Poster
for* FARTHEST NORTH. DR FRIDTJOF NANSEN.
LONDON.
   Nansen stands before the lantern-slide screen.

NANSEN

At your Royal Geographical Society in 1892
I lectured on my plans and heard those learned men
   pooh-pooh
my ideas for my journey and declare it wasn't true
that I could deduce an Arctic current from the seaman's
   oilskin garb
that had drifted from Siberia as far as Julianhaab
in south-west Greenland and so proved the current's flow.
I said there was a current. The RGS said no.
But I've not come back to London to say I told you so!
My success sprang from disaster. I owe a doleful debt
to the debris that had drifted from the doomed *Jeanette*
that sailed from San Francisco to the Bering Strait,
where it foundered, crushed by ice, a not uncommon fate
for ships in the Arctic ice pack. But from this wreck
   came clues.
The RGS said it couldn't change its (I thought rearguard)
   views
if the only evidence it was offered was a pair of oilskin
   trews.
They thought it was effrontery, the most impudent of
   cheeks
to think I'd alter Polar history with a pair of drifting
   breeks.

'And, look at the *Jeanette*,' they said. 'No ship can withstand
the crushing of the pack ice around Franz Josef Land.
When the temperature drops to forty below freezing
the ice pack round the Arctic ship begins its fatal
   squeezing.
and if the expedition meets such predictable defeat
Dr Nansen 's foolish to plan no line of retreat.'
They'd given me a medal for it so I didn't need to boast
I was first to cross Greenland from East coast to West
   coast,
from uninhabited to habited, so 'no line of retreat'
and it was now a strategy I intended to repeat.

   Fram slide goes up on the screen.

FORWARD, FORWARD, Norwegian *Fram* 's the name
on my ship's prow. My heart 's stamped with the same.
And what a ship she proved to be, built with rounded
   sides
so when the groaning ice pack grips its hull it slides
downwards and the *Fram*, instead of cracking, lifts
and, frozen in the ice floes, as I predicted, drifts.

I had the best ship built that ever sailed the Polar Sea
and I left Christiania in 1893.
Some pompous 'expert' said, 'Nansen's going to lose
a lot more than the sailor who lost his oilskin trews.'
The 'experts' said that the ice would mash the *Fram*
to matchwood. I'd be doomed. And . . . and here I am!
in London to present some lantern slides which show
some of my adventures in the Arctic ice and snow.

   A second lantern-slide screen with Fram. *Nansen
   moves to it.*

The 'experts' said that the ice would mash the *Fram*
to matchwood. I'd be doomed. And . . . and here I am!

16

in Newcastle to present some lantern slides which show
some of my adventures in the Arctic ice and snow.

A third and final lantern-slide screen with Fram.
Nansen moves to it.

The 'experts' said that the ice would mash the *Fram*
to matchwood. I'd be doomed. And . . . and here I am!
in Aberdeen to present some lantern slides which show
some of my adventures in the Arctic ice and snow.

All three screens still show the slide of the Fram. *As
Nansen shows his slides they appear simultaneously
on each screen.*

The *Fram* the very day I first felt the huskies pull
my sled towards the Pole. Note the rounded hull.
One of her special features that made her rise above
the pressure of the pack ice when the huge floes push
    and shove
and shatter ships less thoughtfully designed.
She gracefully glides upwards when the glaciers grind.
I left the *Fram* at latitude 84 4
uncertain when I left her if I'd see her any more.
It was March 14th 1895
and I struck out for the Pole determined to survive.
And –

A slide of Nansen's phonogram surrounded by ice.

   – although I had, reluctantly, to leave it on the *Fram*
I had the crew wind up my beloved phonogram
and place it on the ice so that it would play
Eva singing Grieg as the dog-sled pulled away.
This is my wife's voice pouring out her soul
fainter and fainter as I struck out for the Pole,
all art, all music, indeed anything refined
left, and maybe left for ever, far, far, far behind,
except for the poems I'd stored up in my mind.

And –

A slide of Hjalmar Johansen in Arctic furs appears on the screens.

– I want to introduce on this next lantern slide

The lantern-slide images of Johansen speak.

JOHANSEN

Hjalmar Johansen, drunk, depressive, suicide.

Nansen continues, totally unaware of the interruption. The lantern-slide images become still again.

NANSEN

my chosen companion on my quest for the Pole, Hjalmar Johansen!

The lantern-slide images of Johansen speak.

JOHANSEN

The dark side of his soul!

The lantern-slide images of Johansen become still again. Nansen quickly moves the slide image onto one of dogs. The centre screen of the three still has the image of Johansen.

NANSEN

We made thorough preparations for our expedition: dogs, loaded sleds, kayaks, guns and ammunition, chocolate, pemmican, dehydrated soups by Knorr . . .

Nansen breaks off.

I hear you sentimental British, who put their dogs before even other human beings, when I show this slide, say: 'Aw!' In the whole of Europe no other group has sighed so much in the darkness when I've shown this slide of our faithful companions.

The image of Johansen speaks.

JOHANSEN
Tell them how they died!

NANSEN
(*as if not hearing*)
These were our most faithful companions and friends.

JOHANSEN
(*from the screen*)
Tell them how our 'companions' met their ends,
our huskies, our malamutes, our shaggy samoyeds.
Go on!

Nansen stays silent.

I wanted to put bullets through their heads
when they came to the end of their sled-hauling life.
But no! I was ordered to use my Lapland knife
and save bullets for bigger beasts that could provide
more meat.
We gave the chopped-up huskies to the other dogs to
eat.
Dr Nansen's a Darwinian with the stress on win!
We cut them up and fed the lumps to their surviving kin.
You could say that every dog was doubly employed,
as hauler of sled loads and dog's dinner when destroyed.
I doubt if canine qualms make hungry dogs demur
at cannibal consumption of a clapped-out comrade cur.
And maybe dogs have a more Darwinian drive
and gladly eat each other to keep themselves alive.
Maybe more Darwinian than Nansen who, though, likes
to eat
husky blood in blubber as a special breakfast treat!

*Nansen angrily gets rid of the Johansen slide and the
slides of the dogs, and puts up one of a Norwegian
flag flying in a Polar wilderness.*

And that's our flag flying at 86 14,
the farthest northern latitude that anyone had been.
We'd hoped to reach the Pole but the drifting ice terrain
forced us finally to head back south again.
We ate a treat of chocolate, slept, and next day planned
to find the *terra firma* of Franz Josef Land.
We hadn't made the Pole but on this day we could boast
that, of all the people in the world, we were the
    northernmost.

Similar slide goes up with Norwegian flag in colour.

And here's a flag I coloured afterwards by hand
to show that it was Norway's flag that flew in that bleak
    land.
I carried colours in the Arctic which I had to sacrifice
to patch up our holed kayaks to get us through the ice.

But once the midnight sun had set we had to build
a winter hut and store up all the meat we'd killed
to survive the freezing darkness till the spring
made it once more possible to think of travelling.

*Another set of three lantern slides, this time forming a
continuous Polar landscape with, on one, a snow and
ice covered 'hut' as built by Nansen and Johansen
to survive the Arctic winter. On third slide (stage left)
the midnight sun begins to set and Johansen holds
out Nansen's Arctic gear as all the slides fly out
revealing the identical icy wilderness in 3D with a
'hut' and a setting midnight sun and Johansen holding
out Nansen's gear. Johansen helps Nansen into his
Arctic gear.*

NANSEN

This is the sort of layered bear-and-seal-fur gear
you're rarely ever out of as an Arctic pioneer.

Our clothes get blackened, caked with soot and greasy goo
and it gets pretty foetid in the sleeping bag for two.
The only occasions we get our hands and faces clean
is when we shoot a bear –

Johansen shoots his rifle at an offstage bear.

JOHANSEN
>   in all we shot nineteen.

NANSEN
And we can cut it open and do ablutions in the blood
that gushes from its body in a gratefully warm flood.
Our hut is ten feet long and exactly six feet wide.
The walls we made of stone and moss, the roof of
>   walrus hide.
When I stretched my arms out my fingers touch each side.
There's an entrance like a burrow we crawl out and in
like an igloo with a door of double walrus skin.
We'll sleep all hours, twenty out of twenty-four
and we'll be able to sleep singly as we couldn't do before.

The midnight sun sets, leaving moonlit darkness.

Right, Johansen!
>   Our winter lodgings are complete.
I'll be free of your snoring and your fidgeting feet.
We've got long months of Arctic winter to get through
and I won't sleep at all if I've still to sleep with you!
You're always twitching and what's more upsetting
>   you're a
persistently objectionable trombone-volume snorer.
Now we've got our hut constructed, what I really want
>   to do
's divide the bag we've had to share right now into two.
Now we can have our separate spaces, one bag each,
with the cooker in the middle that both of us can reach.
I can't bear to be so close to you when you start to snore.

JOHANSEN
(*under breath*)
And the poetry you keep muttering 's a total bloody bore.

NANSEN
What's that?

JOHANSEN
We should have done this long before.

NANSEN
Not possible in the little tent, too cramped and poky, but
now we can be expansive in our palatial hut.
Not to have to listen to you when you snore and fart!

JOHANSEN
Or to you when you're spouting the poet's putrid art.

NANSEN
What was that, Johansen?

JOHANSEN
I said let's make a start.
It's easy to split it. We'll divide it down the seams.

NANSEN
Tonight I'm looking forward to slightly sweeter dreams.

*They enter the hut. A 'night' elapses. A green Aurora.
Hjalmar Johansen emerges, trembling with cold. Then
after a while Nansen, also shivering, though trying to
hide the fact. Nansen's clothes and face are now as
black and greasy as Johansen's. Neither wants to admit
that they couldn't sleep in their separate sleeping bags.*

NANSEN
Ah, Johansen, slept a good deal better, I've no doubt?

JOHANSEN
Like an innocent baby, sir. Went right out.

NANSEN

Me too. Wonderful not to have to hear you snore.

JOHANSEN

In my own space I slept much better than before.

Pause.

NANSEN

I think you're a liar. You didn't sleep all night.

JOHANSEN

To be honest, Dr Nansen, you're absolutely right.

NANSEN

I was frozen. Didn't sleep a wink. In such sub-zero weather
we don't have a choice. Sew the two bits back together.

Exit Nansen into hut.

JOHANSEN

In separate bags we spent a freezing sleepless night
and there's nothing really for it except glumly reunite.

Exit Johansen into the hut.
The Aurora Borealis with spectacular purple light.
Enter Nansen to contemplate the Aurora. He begins
sketching the phenomenon with a box of pastel crayons.

NANSEN

It's a great relief to escape that farter and that snorer
and get my spirits lifted by the sight of the Aurora.
The sagas say that fire-giant Surt 's the one who plays
this lyre strung with light, this veil of purple rays,
the strings that sparkle in the flames of Muspelheim
that represent to Vikings the end of human time.
The fire-giant Surt plays his luminescent lyre
to serenade the world's end in the final fire.
Surt plucks solemn dirges from the last auroral rays

shimmering for the last men in the world's last days.
But as a modern scientific Viking I know the cooling sun
will make the world's finale a far more frozen one.

*Nansen continues contemplating the Aurora and
sketching.*
*Enter Johansen. He starts picking up the pastels
and testing them.*

What are you doing, Johansen?

JOHANSEN
Seeing if they'll do.

NANSEN
Do for what? Drawing's never interested you.

JOHANSEN
The kayaks are leaking. Your sketching chalk,
ground up and mixed with blubber, 'd make good kayak
    caulk.

NANSEN
Ground up? They're far too precious to me whole
to capture the Aurora that captivates my soul.

JOHANSEN
If you ever want us to escape out of the ice
you'll have to face up to that artistic sacrifice.

NANSEN
I know you took against me because of, I think, the fact
that instead of extra pemmican you noticed that I'd
    packed
my sketching pads and pastels. Do you resent
the life of the finer spirit my pastels represent?

JOHANSEN
The mandate in our packing was, only carry gear
utterly essential to the Polar pioneer,

and for me it wasn't essential, hardly vital
to lug along a phonogram with your wife's song recital.
I'd wanted my accordion and a little *aquavit*,
both essential to my spirit, that you did not permit.

NANSEN

To make you less grudging and embittered I left the
    phonogram
with Eva singing Grieg's songs back on board the *Fram*.

JOHANSEN

You had it playing on the ice as we departed.

NANSEN

I couldn't bear to leave her voice. I was broken-hearted.

JOHANSEN

I know the tune by heart. I heard you play
Eva singing Edvard Grieg almost every day.
I know you're the commander. If you say 'Art supplies
are fundamental', who am I to criticise?
But now, Dr Nansen, I'm afraid you have to choose
between sketching the Aurora or caulking our canoes.
We'll never get through the ice floes if your precious art
    supply
isn't pounded up with blubber to keep our kayaks dry.

NANSEN
(*looking at the Aurora*)
How can you hope to capture that fantastic light
in photographs that show it in only black and white?

*Nansen throws down pastels and flaunts off angrily
back into the hut.*
    *Johansen starts grinding the pastels with great
relish, pounding them rhythmically. An Aurora flashes
spectacularly and dies away.*

25

JOHANSEN

Well, I felt a bit triumphant when his precious art supply
got pounded up with blubber to keep our kayaks dry.
The crayons were essential to caulk the kayak leaks.
We'll need them, I hope, soon, but Nansen's sulked for
     weeks.
I thought it just a ruse he used so he didn't have to talk,
drawing the Aurora with his pretty artist's chalk.
Now the ruse he'll use more of 'll be declaiming verse.
He'll do almost anything so we won't converse.
Reciting poetry! Something he preferred
to speaking to me to whom he scarcely said a word.

Imitating Nansen:

'The only spiritual equivalent I myself have found
to six pounds of beefsteak sun-and-wind-dried to one
     pound
is, Johansen, poetry, the spirit's pemmican,
that nourishes the soul as no other substance can.
Until we escape from here, until that happy day,
the pemmican of poetry will be my spirit's stay.
Poetry, Johansen, not I fancy to your taste,
is now my only consolation in this Arctic waste.'

Exit Johansen into the hut.
     *Time elapses. Another Aurora lights up the sky
briefly and dies.*
     *Nansen pushes the double bear-fur bag out of the
hut.*

NANSEN

This double bear-fur bag that you and I are sharing
stinks of farts and blubber and badly needs an airing.

*Johansen bashes the bag to clear it of ice and the
rhythm gradually becomes that of the metre of the
verse he and Nansen are speaking.*

JOHANSEN

In this double bear-fur bag with its blubber smells and
    farts
I had my reluctant schooling in the skaldic arts.
We had to share the bear-fur bag to keep our bodies warm
and his nocturnal chunterings taught me poetic form.
In this double bear-fur bag where our bodies really stink,
me, I just lay there, desperate, listening, and I think
how much bloody longer till I can get a bloody drink.

*Johansen bangs on the double bear-fur bag to relieve
his frustration.*

And if there was a respite from the sound of verse
the rare conversations were, frankly, a lot worse.
One particular one I remember really fucked my brain.

*Enter Nansen, who surveys the vast icy landscape.
He helps to hold up the fur sleeping bag for Johansen
to bang.*

NANSEN

The whole globe will become like this ice-bound bleak
    terrain!
This icy landscape we endure, great scientists have said,
will be global, universal, once the sun is dead!
You know, Johansen, science prophesies
the whole globe will be polar once the sun's fire dies.
It's a certainty, Johansen, Man cannot rely
on the sun being eternal. One day the sun will die.
Humanity will die with temperatures so low
and it will mean the end of everything we know.
The whole Earth, even the tropics, will finally appear
as white and as frozen as the land around us here.
Then the world will scrabble for sleeping bags like these!
Furless unfortunates will be the first to freeze.

JOHANSEN

But what if humanity could co-operate
and collectively save the doomed globe from this fate?
There's Socialism some men start believing in . . .

NANSEN

Socialism, Johansen, 's pathetic, feminine.

JOHANSEN

Sorry, Dr Nansen, just thought it worth a mention.

NANSEN

Socialism's an inconceivable contravention
of the basic rules of life which, Darwin says, require
that the weaker should always sink beneath the higher.
And when the sun does cool and the last days come,
even if it's not till next millennium,
you can bet your so-called socialists will fight
their erstwhile comrades for food and heat and light.
Until in the end there'll be no way to sustain
life on Earth's frozen surface.

Exit Nansen.

JOHANSEN
                              Yeah, that fucked my brain.
Nansen's idea of chit-chat or bedtime conversation
conjuring up the vision of the globe's annihilation,
I think that that belief of his helped put into my head
that life had no purpose and I was better dead.
The Earth's ultimate extinction! Makes you think
why bother living, struggling, and that drives you to drink.
But he won't permit it here, and it's rather fucking far
to trek across the Arctic to find a bloody bar.

So take a look! This view you've got before you 's how
the whole globe's going to look not too long from now.
The whole globe, seas and cities, Paris, Berlin, Rome,

the frozen neighbourhood about your London home –
Hampstead, Islington, the West End, the South Bank,
all a featureless, completely frozen blank.
It robs the heart of purpose, saps the spirit's goals
to know the globe in its entirety will end up like the poles.
Even Darwin's fittest 'll be no better placed
for survival than the weakest in the final frozen waste.
The fittest will seem feeble and the fittest of the fit
like 'Farthest North' Nansen and the Arctic Inuit,
used as they may be to the Polar ice and snow,
will find that even they die at temperatures so low.

When I walk this ice and snow I'm inside my own brain
which is a similar barren ice-bound bleak terrain.
But if that bastard had allowed it and I could only pour a
nice big glass of *aquavit* I'd make my own Aurora,
and feel the fiery spirit give me a certain glow
deep in the grateful gut, and fuck the ice and snow.
But the only bit of warmth I'll get round here is back
with bloody Nansen in this bloody bear-fur sack.

> *Exit Johansen, pulling the double bear-fur bag behind*
> *him into hut.*
>   *Arctic winter over. Sun. Enter Nansen and Johansen*
> *from hut. They start to leave and set off dragging*
> *kayaks.*

When we have to use our kayaks when it's too wet to
    walk
you'll be glad I used your crayons to make the kayak
    caulk.
Patched with pastels I pounded to make a pitchy glue
instead of pretty pictures of auroras that you drew.
If I hadn't done it then the kayaks would've sunk
and you'd never get a chance to compete with Edvard
    Munch.
And look, the last of these auroras –

NANSEN
Aurorae!

JOHANSEN
Whatever! I'll remember them until the day I die.

NANSEN
That day could well be sooner than you think.

JOHANSEN
I refuse to die till I've had a good stiff drink.
I've dreamed for all this time about that first big dram.

NANSEN
And I of home, my armchair, and my phonogram.
And reuniting with our comrades from the *Fram*.

They travel, hauling the kayaks. They stop.
    Time elapses. Johansen fires his rifle at some animal
for food. Sound of dogs barking.

Johansen, barking dogs. And barking dogs mean men.
Perhaps we are going to see our motherland again.

A mass of Norwegian flags. Fram *comes into*
Christiania Harbour projected onto Olivier shutters.
    Sound of brass bands and cheering.
    Enter Gilbert Murray, and Sybil Thorndike in her
dressing gown.

GILBERT MURRAY
Home to brass bands and cheering on the Christiania
quays.

SYBIL THORNDIKE
Thank God, you didn't want me sliding in on skis!
Even I, not a veggie, soon had quite enough
of the bears' brains and the blubber and the *Boys Own*
    Paper stuff.
I'm so relieved you didn't force me to appear

in that positively unflattering greasy polar gear.
For one awful moment I thought you'd brought me
    back
to enter Larry's theatre in some ghastly anorak.
Long ago I made myself a golden rule:
never play a character whose costume's a kagool.
It must have made you nauseous, the meat whiffs from
    the hut.

GILBERT MURRAY

I feared they'd start gutting seals so kept my eyes tight
    shut.
I'll watch the crowds cheer Nansen, Nansen being feted,
but would rather not watch Johansen get inebriated.
Nansen has an audience with King Oscar.

JOHANSEN
(shouting off)
                            Forget that Oscar shit!
Christiania will see me quaffing aquavit.

GILBERT MURRAY

Everywhere in Europe there was a Nansen 'boom'
as Johansen's dram indulgences brought him nearer doom.
For a short time he broke his dependence on the 'dram'
and Nansen got Johansen back on board the Fram
as a member of Amundsen's expedition crew,
a chance the bibulous beggar belligerently blew
when, after immoderate imbibing, and an insubordinate
    act,
Captain Amundsen had Johansen summarily sacked.
Which put paid to the ambition the doomed dram-bibber
    nursed
of triumphing over Nansen by reaching a Pole first.
The dismissal turned him into a melancholy loner
stoked up on aquavit and always short of kroner.
Nansen's northern record lasted only for five years

before being superseded by other Polar pioneers.
He began to drift directionless into dark grudge and grief.

SYBIL THORNDIKE
Sounds like it needs me to bring some light relief.

Exit Gilbert Murray and Sybil Thorndike.
Enter Nansen to chair and phonogram.

NANSEN
I was the man reached latitude 86 14,
the farthest north that any man had ever been,
but the record only lasted five brief years
before being overtaken by new Polar pioneers.
The double, hurtful irony 's that what were once my ships
helped Amadeo and Amundsen to accomplish my eclipse.
Jason, the sealer I sailed to Greenland in, became
Amadeo's *Pole Star* and put paid to my fame.
My *Jason* got Amadeo further North than me.
I'd reached 86 14 and Amadeo 33.
Twenty miles only, but twenty's all it needed
for me to know my record was safely superseded.

Reads telegram:

OBJECTIVE REACHED STOP AMUNDSEN. That put a
    stop to me
being at the pinnacle of polar history.
My own Arctic achievements seem more and more remote
now Amundsen's reached the South Pole using *Fram*,
    my boat.
Amundsen reached the South Pole with such apparent ease
because he used my system of sledges, dogs and skis.
I was once more among crowds on the Christiania quay,
crowds cheering their new hero, but this time it's not me.

Fram once more sails into Christiania Harbour with
brass bands and waving flags.

Enter Hjalmar Johansen, drunk.

JOHANSEN

It was almost, but for Amundsen, me the quayside throng
would have been cheering in the *Fram* where I belong,
me, the second time *Fram* voyager Norwegians would
    applaud
but *Fram* sailed up the fjord and I was not on board.
Amundsen, the bastard who sacked me, used your boat
for his conquest of the South Pole and is going to demote
the name of Nansen on the roster of the great
when the fickle voice of fame finds newer names to
    celebrate.
For five years everywhere you've been cheered and feted.
What future after Amundsen now you've been relegated?
A Darwinist with the stress on win. So what happens
    when you lose?
Does it make you open to more sympathetic views?
Can you look into your heart and find some empathy
with those destined to be losers, like me, like me, like me?

Nansen in his depressed reverie puts on the
phonogram: his wife Eva singing Grieg. He listens.

NANSEN

Eva! whose voice I still listen to on the phonogram
as I did in the Arctic winter before we left the *Fram*.
It consoles me to listen. Though she's dead I still need her
though the consolation I need now is way beyond all
    lieder.
With the globe entirely penetrated, both poles mapped,
it leaves me with my energy completely sapped.
The conquered poles have paralysed my initiative
and without my urge for action I find it hard to live.
I feel surrounded by ice floes but this time they're all
    black,
implacable, crushing, and my heart's about to crack.

33

The heart I thought was like the *Fram* is more like the
    Jeanette,
crushed by the icy darkness though not quite shattered yet.
Despair makes me dispirited, listless and unmanned
as much as poor Johansen –

    The sound of Eva's singing grows.
      Bang. It's Johansen, whom we see shoot himself.
    A great spurt of blood spouts onto the ice.
    Enter Ghost of Johansen.

JOHANSEN
                – who died by his own hand.
You thought it and I did it, as if at your command!
I blew my brains out with the very gun I shot
bears and seals and foxes for our supper pot.
Like the pennants of blood sprayed from our polar prey,
my brains were hauled and flown in exactly the same way.
I've seen it so many times but now the flag that's flown
and the brains that burst out with it are no beast's but
    my own,
a blast of flapping banner, a gory banderole,
a bloodflag with the blazon of my brain-sick blackened
    soul.
That bloodflag of my suicide should be planted to be seen
by all who reach the wilderness of 86 14.

I put into practice what you scarcely dared to think.
You want solace for your sorrow, but Johansen quaffs
    the drink.
You saw the unmapped places conquered one by one
and felt your life was pointless but Johansen fires the gun.
You thought the desperate thought. I did the deed.
I didn't damn my spirit so Nansen's could be freed,
freed to find some other soul-fulfilling goal
to compensate your spirit for the conquest of the Pole.
This act of mine, this suicide, it's meant always to bind

your thoughts and my thoughts together in one mind.
When I blew my brains out it was not to make you free
but bind you even closer to the ghost that once was me.

NANSEN

My spirit was almost crushed but like the *Fram* in frozen
    floes,
gripped by despair and darkness, withstood their force,
    and rose.
The sun will cool, the Earth will freeze, that simple fact,
though it paralysed Johansen, now makes me want to act.
The Earth will be one huge Arctic and man's endeavour
disappear beneath the ice and lost to time for ever.
You've got to steel your mind and heart to gaze into that
    void
and then commit to action and be busily employed.
We create our purpose, we create our goal.
And now it's helping humankind, not reaching the
    North Pole.
Science says its certain, Johansen's desperate reaction
was drink, depresssion, suicide, mine was always *action*.

   Exit Nansen.

JOHANSEN

My last action was the fatal shot, but if he acts or no
everywhere that Nansen goes my ghost will also go.
My ghost swears never to leave Nansen's side
and haunt the lapsed Darwinian with my suicide,
League of Nations Commissioner for Refugees!
Not a post a Darwinian can fulfil with any ease!
I'll be there to denounce the doctor for his Darwinian
    defection.
It's not Nature now but Nansen who is doing the selection.
Now that he's adopted his international role
he's jettisoned those laws of life we clung to at the Pole.
Johansen's ghost returns to put back in his ear

all he wants suppressing in his new world-wide career.
I'll remind him, ex-Darwinian, what he drummed into
    my brain –
the strong should flourish, the weak go down the drain.
He's a 'humanitarian' now, no longer an explorer
and he's off to New York to watch a ballet called *Aurora*.

Sound of an orchestra tuning up.
Gold proscenium, red velvet curtains fly in.

Composer, designer, dancer, each a Russian émigré,
came on so-called 'Nansen passports' to the USA.
But did any Nansen-passport-saved Pied Piper with his
    flute
do anything to civilise the European brute?
Although the bloody ballet's something I can't bear
I want to sour his delight with a dose of my despair.
Despair a gift from you that I will give you back
to remind you of the darkness when we shared one
    sleeping sack.

Exit Johansen.
    Enter Gilbert Murray through red curtains. He
    tiptoes downstage to lean over the 'orchestra pit'.

GILBERT MURRAY
Maestro! Maestro! For the purpose of my play
could you give us a rendition of only part of the ballet?

Spotlight on curtain. The head of Sybil Thorndike
pokes through.

SYBIL THORNDIKE
So before I appear there's a whole ballet to sit through?

GILBERT MURRAY
I've already told the orchestra a part of it will do.

SYBIL THORNDIKE
Then me?

Yes, you, and me, and Nansen, London, 1922.
We'll meet him and others and sit in on their discussions
on how they can publicise the plight of starving Russians.

Exit Gilbert Murray through red curtains.

SYBIL THORNDIKE
(*to Gilbert Murray*)
I can't wait much longer!

To audience:

Well, at least he's let you know
you won't have long to wait before the real star of the
show.

Exit Sybil Thorndike.
The curtain rises.
*The scene is the same Arctic wilderness, except it is
now framed by a gilded proscenium arch for the ballet
of the Aurora Borealis, a ballet that should seem as if
composed by Stravinsky, designed by Chagall and
danced by Pavlova, all of whom were recipients at
one time or another of a Nansen passport.*
*There are also two theatre boxes. In one sits
Fridtjof Nansen.*

*The ballet ends. Dancer takes her call. Curtsies to
Nansen in box. Nansen presents a bouquet of red
roses to the Dancer. Applause. Curtain.*
Exit Nansen, revealing Johansen behind.
*Johansen changes the box into one at the Bolshoi
with hammer and sickle over the old double eagle of
the Tsar.*

JOHANSEN
Now he's going back to Russia to tour the famine zone
acting as if he's feeding the millions on his own.

37

My ghost'll be on his trail, and always ready to remind
Nansen the Darwinist of beliefs he's left behind.

Johansen sees ARA Men entering their box.

On furlough from the famine for a bit of Moscow play,
here come the youthful heroes of the ARA,
the American Relief Administration,
doing even more than Nansen to relieve starvation,
having time off from the famine, a free box at the Bolshoi.
Each one, except their Moscow boss, nobbut a green boy
from the boondocks of Iowa, Wisconsin, Illinois.

*Three ARA Men, Stuart Shaw, James Callaghan and
William H. Rutland, enter their box in the middle of
a discussion which continues while they doff their fur
hats and coats.*

STUART SHAW
What you're saying's wrong. If you think that you're a
fool.
Finishing the famine won't prop up Bolshie rule.

JAMES CALLAGHAN
Hoover wouldn't do it if he thought that was true
and I wouldn't be here helping . . .

WILLIAM H. RUTLAND
                                    and nor would you.
The one thing that's been paradoxically essential 's
Hoover's utterly impeccable anti-Bolshevik credentials.
Herbert Hoover's always, always, you know, presumed
that the folly of communism 's ultimately doomed.
I've always understood it was Hoover's attitude
that the Russian Revolution was a riot about food.

STUART SHAW
Somewhere the basic ethos of Hoover's ARA 's
if you want to stop Bolshevism, food's the best of ways.

The American Relief Administration 's a manoeuvre
typical of the genius of our Chief, Herbert Hoover.

WILLIAM H. RUTLAND

He's had to square our save-the-starving mission
with US official policy of complete non-recognition.
The Bolshies' bungling and the bureaucratic mess
would be seen in total contrast with ARA success
and efficiency, all down to the Chief,
Herbert Hoover, the genius of famine relief.

JAMES CALLAGHAN

The ARA makes Bolshevism seem like a dead loss.

STUART SHAW

Here comes Sheldon, guys, the Moscow bureau boss.

*An older man, Sheldon, enters the box and struggles
out of his furs.*

SHELDON

Thank God tonight's an opera. I've had it with ballet.
Not that Isadora does it in the normal way.
I saw her here in Moscow perform to a great crowd.
If I wasn't among VIPs I'd've laughed out loud.
She danced *The Russian Famine*. What arrogance
for this podgy passé prancer to do a *Famine* dance.
She pranced about in skimpy silks to a Scriabin *étude*.
All I can say is, thank Christ she wasn't dancing nude!
Rolls of blubber round the belly somehow don't symbolise
starvation on the Volga, not to mention chubby thighs!
I thought, for Christ's sake, keep all the arts away
from the kind of work we try to do in the ARA,
especially preserve us from the art of the ballet.
So thank God it's an opera we got tickets for tonight.

Hey, look behind the hammer and sickle of the USSR,
you can still see the great gold double eagle of the Tsar.
And that's the Tsar's own box! Oh my Gawd!

A Man in furs enters the Tsar's box.

Look, there!

Man in box removes furs and reveals himself as Nansen.

JAMES CALLAGHAN
Who is it?

SHELDON
Nansen! Just wait, they'll all applaud.

Long applause and cheers from unseen audience.
Nansen bows and waves.

WILLIAM H. RUTLAND
I had a letter from my folks back home, by the way,
saying Nansen was responsible for improving our ballet.
They saw one in New York entitled *The Aurora*
and said it owed so much to Nansen the explorer-
turned-humanitarian and were full of praise
about the boost to arts there'd been with all the émigrés
on Nansen passports, glad, no doubt, to have fled
the famine here in Russia and the diet of dung bread.

SHELDON
I've a meeting in London, England, with our very man,
a kinda famine summit for this year's master plan.
We'll be meeting in a coupla days to sum up and review
our Russian famine strategy for 1922.
The other agencies, *Save the Children*, *Society of Friends*,
who are giving us what help they can to achieve our ends,
they'll be there represented by a Miss Jebb and Miss Fry
at whom I've no doubt Nansen will be rolling the old eye!
And there'll be Gilbert Murray, a League of Nations type,
who'll probably contribute some idealistic tripe.
Hoover's American Relief Administration 's
going to achieve far more than any League of Nations.
The ARA has set up an efficient working model

for famine relief; we don't need League of Nations
     twaddle.
And this Professor Murray so I'm told 's a drama freak.
Drama would be bad enough but his kind 's ancient
     Greek!
He's partial to Greek drama in his own translations
and more naive than Nansen about the League of Nations.
Murray 's escorting, as his special lady guest,
some broad called Sybil Thorndike, said to be the best
actress of her generation. God! We're gonna have to sit
and listen to her declaiming ancient tragic shit.

JAMES CALLAGHAN

Don't envy you that. Can't imagine anything worse
than have to hear some British broad spouting fucking
     verse!

*Applause from Bolshoi audience as Conductor enters
to begin the overture.*

SHELDON

Oop, here comes the conductor. I dunno. I dunno
what good's going to come from being at this show.
I'd better shut up. It's about to start.
Once you've seen the famine you wonder about art!

Applause. Conductor. Overture.
   *Overture finishes. Red velvet curtain of the Bolshoi
goes up to reveal Eglantyne Jebb watching the Save
the Children Fund film of the Russian famine.*
   *It ends, then she switches on the lights of a room of
her house turned into a kind of campaign centre, and
she broods about the film until the spool of film runs
out of the projector.*
   The gold proscenium flies out.
   *Sheldon in London on his way to a meeting with
Fridtjof Nansen, Gilbert Murray, Sybil Thorndike,
Eglantyne Jebb and Ruth Fry.*

SHELDON

Though we've both worked on the famine, I regret
that Nansen and I have not, till now in London, ever met.
Nansen, Miss Jebb, Miss Fry the Quaker, and the prof –
what's his name, Professor Murray! I shouldn't scoff,
I guess, and I know he's also a League of Nations man
who is earnest and committed to doing what he can,
but how can Greek drama be of any earthly use
to us in famine work? OK, so maybe I'm a bit obtuse,
but I figure he's got that actress Sybil-something in tow
because he's planning on performing some after-dinner
    show.
The reality in this canister is gonna supersede
All that poetry-spouting, Sybil Thorndike breed.
God spare us goddam culture when the point of our
    discussion 's
the quickest way to save the lives of millions of Russians.

Nansen towers above us, although the ARA
feeds millions more than he could in a single day.
We do all the goddam work and he gets the applause.

*Enter Nansen, Gilbert Murray, Sybil Thorndike,
Eglantyne Jebb and Ruth Fry.*

SHELDON

Dr Nansen, my hero, the inspiration of our cause!
I feel so honoured to meet you here today

NANSEN

You're working on the Volga with the ARA?

SHELDON

Yes, sir, Sheldon, and we're all inspired by you.

NANSEN

That would be wonderful if it were only true.

SHELDON

How could you ever doubt it? Surely you're aware

42

of how you're applauded for the work you've done out
    there?
You've taught the world compassion, the indifferent to
    care.

EGLANTYNE JEBB

The indifferent need to learn to care a good deal more
and that, dear Dr Nansen, 's what your Queen's Hall
    lecture's for.
Mr Sheldon, pleased to meet you. Miss Jebb, Eglantyne!

NANSEN

We all have a favourite flower, and the eglantine,
with its slightly timid beauty, happens to be mine.

GILBERT MURRAY

Miss Jebb, your bloodstream must be full of ancient
    Greece.

To all:

She is the greatest editor of Sophocles's niece.
Miss Jebb, you may be, but our guests are unaware
I succeeded your uncle Richard to the Glasgow chair.

EGLANTYNE JEBB

I know my uncle Richard was your predecessor
in the Chair of Greek at Glasgow. I welcome you,
    Professor!

GILBERT MURRAY
(to Sheldon, the ARA man)

I'm Professor Murray.

Introduces Sybil Thorndike.

         And this Sybil Thorndike, a sensation
as Hecuba . . .

SYBIL THORNDIKE
in Dr Murray's own translation!

43

GILBERT MURRAY

She is what you Americans refer to as a 'star'.

SHELDON

I've not had the privilege of seeing you so far.
Perhaps you'd grace the evening with a recitation.
Sheldon! American Relief Administration.

SYBIL THORNDIKE

Good evening, Mr Sheldon, I think your ARA
and Dr Nansen do far more than any play.

EGLANTYNE JEBB

Sybil, we all try our best, each in our own way.
We all look forward to hearing your ideas tonight
how theatre can help the starving in their sorry plight.

To everybody:

Everybody! We need to check if the nationwide
     discussion 's
swinging in our favour in the matter of the Russians.
Let's review the papers then we'll go next door to eat.
Dr Nansen, there's one more guest for you to meet –

Eglantyne Jebb ushers Ruth Fry before Nansen.

A guest whom I think you may already know.

NANSEN
(approving the look of Ruth Fry)
I'm not sure that I do. But would dearly wish it so!

EGLANTYNE JEBB

I can't believe you've not already met.

NANSEN
(using his doubt to look Ruth Fry over)
I don't think that we have. Much to my regret.

EGLANTYNE JEBB

Ruth Fry! Of *The Friends*! She was on the Volga too.

NANSEN

One meets so many people, but I'm sorry I missed you.

RUTH FRY

Dr Nansen! It's an honour. How do you do?

EGLANTYNE JEBB

So now we'll review the papers and dream up means
   to try
to publicise the famine before more millions die.

Gilbert Murray holds up the Greek mask.

GILBERT MURRAY

Before we get too deeply into our deliberation
I should like to make beforehand a little presentation.
Dr Nansen, this gift is for you. The tragic mask!
To give you inspiration for your momentous task.
Inspiration from the ancient past, to help you stir and
   shake
those who need persuading, for the starving millions' sake,
to lend first their attention, then their financial aid.

NANSEN

I'll need it. Europe's far from easy to persuade.

GILBERT MURRAY

The tragic mask for me has come to symbolise
the art of facing horror with always-open eyes.
No eyelids on a tragic mask. It has no choice but see
and its mouth is always open to utter poetry.

NANSEN

The mouth of starvation is always open too.

GILBERT MURRAY

But our mask's ancient eloquence will help inspire you
to move the world to end the famine, but I think it's only
   right
that you should receive it from our theatre's leading light.

From the bottom of my heart and from thespians
   nationwide
who would all desert the stage to do service at your side,
from all of us in theatre who do the little that we can
our token of regard to a most inspiring man.
Please accept this present as a mark of our esteem.

Nansen contemplates the mask and Sybil Thorndike.
He puts it to his face and screams very loud. Everyone
is shocked. Nansen laughs.

NANSEN

It reminds me of my countryman Edvard Munch's *The*
   Scream.
For well nigh thirty years the picture's haunted me,
painted as it was by Munch in 1893,
the same year, indeed almost to the day,
the *Fram* went down the fjord about to sail away.
There's a boat in the background and I think there I am
at the start of my adventure in the departing *Fram.*
It looks like Christiania, but the earth, the sea, the sky
are all vibrating with the violence of the cry.
And since being in the Volga I have terrifying dreams
of the open mouths of hunger and the open mouths of
   screams.
In the Volga there are millions of open mouths like these
who need substantial sustenance, not your Euripides.

GILBERT MURRAY

We've raised money and subscribers to the League of
   Nations
by playing the most popular of my Euripides translations,
The Trojan Women with Sybil in the lead.

NANSEN

                        Murray, yes.
But do you really think poetry's the right thing to address

the horrors we are witnessing in times like these,
horrors quite unknown to your friend Euripides?
You know I value poetry quite as much as you:
I survived the Arctic winter by reciting poems I knew,
but could your Greek tragedians, even if they speak
the brilliant English you found for all their Greek,
ever hope to accomplish a poetical narration
of the plight of millions threatened by starvation?
Surely even your tragedians would be bound to fail
to put into poetry a horror on this scale.

GILBERT MURRAY

I'm sure they could. O how I wish that I
really had the talent to give the task a try.
But as a certain someone 's been unkind enough to say,
poetry's not Professor Murray's principal forte.
and many agree with a certain someone's views
on the outmoded melodies of Gilbert Murray's Muse.

EGLANTYNE JEBB

I'd like to begin with what I'm certain you all here
will regard as yet another crazy Eglantyne idea!
What we need at *Save the Children* is a way
that can communicate the horror that language can't
    convey.
Can you imagine, Dr Nansen, your slide-projection screen
as a permanent mural in a crowded works canteen?
What would happen to the world if lantern slides could be
projected into people's homes while they were having tea?
If these actualities could be seen by the whole nation
surely it would mean an end to the horrors of starvation.
If we had a sort of visual version of the telephone
with every household owning a small screen of its own,
I know it seems far-fetched but I know that we'd persuade
people with a 'vision phone' to contribute to aid.
If only we could *see* like we hear on radio,

a wireless that as well as tell could also show.
There'd be no more starvation like this in Saratov.

GILBERT MURRAY
Eglantyne, they might just simply switch it off.

EGLANTYNE JEBB
(*picks up newspaper*)
Look here! We've used this drawing to juxtapose
half-naked Volga starving to our sort in fine clothes.
But my committee thought I'd gone too far when I
    proposed
far more shocking contrasts to be juxtaposed:
a peasant, next to a family weighed down with Christmas
    shopping,
excavating strands of straw from a steaming carthorse
    dropping.
'Good taste' forbids it. 'Good taste' 's my worst frustration.
What on earth is 'tasteful' about extreme starvation?
We at *Save the Children* haven't shied from the technique
that advertising uses, letting pictures speak.

She picks up another paper.

We'll have this advert in the paper. The headline's going
    to say
in large capitals: DOOMED TO DIE ON XMAS DAY.
In the short time it takes to munch a Michaelmas mince pie
a hundred starving Russian mites are going to surely die.
If I had my way, I'd dump all that good taste and adopt
shock tactics that are certain to get starvation stopped.
One day, not now, but one day when we can
show the horrors of Samara and Saratov and Kazan
in all their ghastly colour and hear the children's cries,
we'll succeed in ending famine. I hate this compromise.

NANSEN
'Compromise is Satan's work.' Henrik Ibsen, *Brand*!

EGLANTYNE JEBB
Yes, dear Dr Nansen, I know you understand.

RUTH FRY
Of course it has to be admitted that the most acute distress
is not in Russia but in Cornwall, or so says the *Express*.

She picks up the Express.

Look, columns on Cornwall and the paper's damning
on the Volga which they call 'the other famine'.
Lord Beaverbrook's *Express*! There's a pernicious *exposé*
of you at *Save the Children* in the *Express* every day!
Beaverbrook's readers have their tender feelings torn
by unemployed tin-miners in Redruth or Camborne.

EGLANTYNE JEBB
Our rubbishers on Beaverbrook's *Express* contend
that we (that of course means me) at *Save the Children*
    spend
more on salaries and adverts and administration
than goes in the end to Russia to relieve starvation.
Our patron, the Archbishop of Canterbury no less,
has also been vilified in this week-old *Express*.

Reads from the Express:

'The Archbishop would do best to distribute
charitable food to his Lambeth destitute.
Never mind the Volga, he only needs to take his walks
in the slums of Lambeth to see where Famine stalks.'

NANSEN
And this is me from an issue of last week.
As a kind of culmination to their usual critique
of how unbelievable my last reports had been,
the *Express* invites its readers to judge between
the words of a 'foreigner' (that's me!) and what's been
    written

by 'an *Express* journalist born and bred in Britain'.
We've got to use cunning and contrive new ways to
  counteract
the Beaverbrook *Express* and show the famine's fact.

When they attacked the famine as a Bolshevistic lie
all I could do to silence them was *verbally* deny,
but from now on in Russia the photographs I take
will be the proof I need to show the famine isn't fake.
Express readers will believe Beaverbrook's foul lies
until they see the starving before their very eyes,
and it's that in the end that has forced me to decide
I had once more to resort to the realistic slide.
Perhaps 'movies' will become the more realistic means
of convincing an audience they're seeing actual scenes.
Miss Jebb, or may I call you Eglantyne,
it happens to be a favourite flower of mine,
you at Save the Children are there already, are you not?
Your director and myself were (what's the parlance?) . . .

SHELDON

'shot'.

EGLANTYNE JEBB

We'll watch our film and Mr Sheldon's later. Film's a new
and important way to get our message through.
Oue film's been shown already on more than one occasion.
A wonderful new weapon in our armoury of persuasion.
So, Dr Nansen, I agree that you are right
to be showing slides of horror in your talk tomorrow
  night.
I think we'll find such methods will be more and more
  employed –
the saviour of the starving may well be celluloid.

RUTH FRY

But sometimes it *is* possible the camera can lie.

50

NANSEN

Don't tell that to Beaverbrook, I beg of you, Miss Fry!
Since his malice against Bolsheviks is bitter and unending
Beaverbrook 'll claim the corpses were pretending!

EGLANTYNE JEBB

The *Manchester Guardian* yesterday published a review
of our fund's *Famine* film, and a very good one too,
by their cinematographic critic, C. A. Lejeune,
though her article shows a great deal more concern
for new films in full colour not like ours in monochrome,
nonetheless she grants that our images
(*Reads.*)   '*bring home
as words can never* (note that never!) *bring
the dread and the hopelessness of Volga suffering.*'
And this is from the *Daily Telegraph*, 20th Jan:
(*Reads.*) '*No film has shown such horror since cinema
    began.*'
The other films she writes about though must make ours
    much duller
as these are made with a process that shows things in
    full colour.
Every day they're developing more brilliant technique
like the colour cinematograph shown here just last
    week.

SHELDON

Any increase in reality surely must be good!
In the films of the future blood will look like blood.
Movie makers won't have their accustomed monochrome
    recourse,
when they want blood depicted, to Hershey's chocolate
    sauce.

EGLANTYNE JEBB

But to be honest I still think monochrome
might be the best medium to get our message home.

I think our film makes the Russians' desperate plight
look even more harrowing in plain old black and white.

SHELDON
Yes, pictures are getting better by the day.
We've had this modest movie made about the ARA.
It shows our American Relief Administration
working to rescue the Russians from starvation.
It concentrates less on horror more on gratitude displayed
by the starving of the Volga for US relief and aid.

RUTH FRY
I was in Samara when some of it was made.
Yes, I was in the region and saw it being 'shot'.
But can you call it reality? Unfortunately not!

SHELDON
Miss Fry! Whatever can you possibly mean?

RUTH FRY
I'm referring above all to one particular scene.
Your ARA 'movie', had control of it been mine
(and I'm not sure if you'll support me, Eglantyne),
there are certain aspects of it where I'd've drawn the line.
I saw the cameraman take a scoop of corn and throw
grains precious to the watchers in the melting snow.
The seed corn they'd seen him so casually scatter
was for them a literally life and death matter.
He then filmed the starving children (surely questionable
    taste)
feverishly searching so not one grain went to waste,
fossicking the slushy ice to fish up every grain,
and your man at his camera, when I ventured to complain,
simply shrugged and said to me, 'That's movies, honey.'

Sheldon laughs.

I confess I didn't find this observation funny.

Then with another shrug I watched him lean
back towards his lens and shoot exactly the same scene.
Then if he wanted peasants kissing food-relievers' feet
and didn't get the image and wanted a repeat
your cameraman discovered they co-operated more
if food supplies were doled out after not before.
Anyone who's had to live on dung and pounded roots
didn't see a problem in being asked to kiss your boots.
But you begin to suspect that something's less than true
when you see a starving peasant waiting for his cue
to kneel down at the feet of ARA relievers, then,
If his fawning wasn't fulsome, be forced to kneel again.
All I want to ask you is, do you believe this is the way
you'll promote what are the real achievements of the
    ARA?

SHELDON

Yes, they're real achievements, that no one can deny
though there are detractors (and the Bolsheviks!) who try.
They're the sort of achievements other agencies resent.
Let's remember the ARA contributes up to 91%
of all aid sent to Russia now in 1922.
And Miss Jebb, if I may make use of your machine,
I'd like to show us guys in action, life size, on the screen.
Not that I undervalue what both you ladies do.
Miss Jebb's *Save the Children*, and Quakers like Miss Fry
have supplied the other 10% we can't (as yet) supply.
And you, sir, Dr Nansen, the famine's leading light,
the beacon of benevolence beaming through the night.

RUTH FRY

The point I really feel I have to make
is, how is the suffering truthful when he has to stage
    his 'take'?
I only bring this up to show you can't rely
on film as truth, and that the camera can lie.

So perhaps Professor Murray's right that words can sway
more than so-called reality captured in this way.

EGLANTYNE JEBB

Professor Murray would prefer that moving pictures speak
(and even better I imagine if they spoke in ancient Greek!)
but sadly so far they've not perfected that technique.

GILBERT MURRAY

But I fear I find it, I might almost say, obscene
to have such shocking pictures projected on a screen.
But then I'm a fuddy-duddy and not at all *au fait*
with all the modern methods available today.

EGLANTYNE JEBB

But film is the direction our campaign should take.
Anything's worth trying for those little children's sake.
Does the means matter if, by shocking, we persuade
the otherwise reluctant to give cash to famine aid?

GILBERT MURRAY

Eglantyne, sorry. I simply can't agree.
For me the most persuasive means is always poetry.
(And I suspect your uncle Richard would think the same
    as me!)
A messenger who's thought about the things he's seen
and not an unmediated image thrown on to a screen,
shows a human mind and heart 's had time to brood
on the witnessed horror sometimes of such a magnitude
it's too overwhelming to take on, a monstrous theme
betrayed by any utterance less violent than a scream . . .
Sometimes you will see that a Greek poet puts in cries,
cries not in metre, like *pheu* or, more frequently, *ai-ai*s.
These are 'extrametrical' – that is, emotional signs
of the inexpressible anguish that generates the lines.
It's as if the messenger were allowed a sort of token
    scream

54

to show the level of the agony behind the measured
    theme.
The cries indicate the inarticulate degree
of suffering inexpressible outside of poetry.
I know I may appear a rather obsessive sort of bore
but it's this that poetry was invented for
to give focus to our suffering and to our pain
and the more it's done through language the more we'll
    stay humane.
Reliance on devices like the photograph and slide
will lead, I rather fear, to linguistic suicide.
We must keep on challenging language to engage
with all we suffer from in this new modern age.
If it doesn't have the words we must challenge it to find
new ones that will measure up to the disasters of mankind.
I think we fall into a deep defeatist trap
to regard poetry superseded by the slide show or the snap!
If it's to a modern appliance that you must go
I would sooner place my trust in the power of radio.
You know, I genuinely believe that I have often seen
vivider pictures on the wireless than the screen.

SYBIL THORNDIKE
I know you've told me, Gilbert, Greek tragedians could,
had they wished to, like us, use buckets of stage blood.
They weren't theatrically backward, so why didn't they?
I know you think it's because they'd found a better way.

GILBERT MURRAY
The messenger speech. A messenger speech
reaches depths in the heart mere pictures never reach.
If the messenger's on target, the mind's eye of the hearer
more than vision itself brings horror even nearer.

EGLANTYNE JEBB
Dr Nansen's photographs no Beaverbrook newshound
despite his devious efforts can possibly confound.

GILBERT MURRAY

The next time there are millions of starving mouths to feed
you'll need to boost the voltage to give the shock you need
to waken up the conscience, and the next time even more
shocking illustrations of a famine or of war.
You have to face it, most people hate to look
at horrors and will react like Beaverbrook.
Which is why I think that your campaign can reach
more people through persuasive (i.e. poetic) speech.

NANSEN

So, Dr Murray, are you only recommending verse
as a means of emptying a charitable purse?

RUTH FRY

Dr Murray, Miss Thorndike, don't you have a way
to enact a person dying in a dramatic play?

GILBERT MURRAY

Miss Thorndike can advise us, Sybil, can you not?

RUTH FRY

Yes, but I don't mean pretending to be shot
or stabbed, and fall down and hold the breath
and adopt the total immobility of death.
Supposing it's starvation an actor chose to play
he'd have to fast for months to get to look that way.
There is scarcely a gram of flesh beneath the skin.
It would take you months of fasting to look as thin
if you were to play the Hecuba of Buzuluk.

SYBIL THORNDIKE

But a portrayal involves far more than how I look!
The words, my empathy, the feelings of my heart
are far more important when I play a part.
All we need are the right lines and imagination
and even a well-fed actor can portray starvation.

SHELDON

Dancing's sure a no-no. I can tell you that.
Saw Isadora Duncan dance the famine. She was fat.
I know she's an artiste of huge worldwide esteem
but she took the Russian famine as her balletic theme.
No matter how much besotted ballet-buffs respect her
her present bulk's not suitable to dance a starving spectre.
She pranced about in skimpy silks to a Scriabin *étude*.
but didn't seem to me like one deprived of food.
In extreme times I doubt we need ballet or a play
but practical men like Nansen here and Hoover's ARA.
In the dire straits of famine there's not much call for
    dancing.
Better Hoovers's ARA and Dr Fridtjof Nansen!
If I may project it and you'd all take a seat.
our film proves theatricals are sort of obsolete.

NANSEN
(to Gilbert Murray)

Nor could your Hecuba, Miss Thorndike, begin to
    audition
to speak for millions in the throes of malnutrition.
I fear even your star actress scarcely qualifies
to be a starving woman despite her slender size.
Though eminently talented and divinely svelte,
Sybil's hardly starving.

SYBIL THORNDIKE
                        But I'd know how she felt!

I don't see why an actress, even one that's overweight,
isn't up to imagining a starving woman's fate!

NANSEN

Dear lady, I'm sure your tragic talent's great,
but even you seem portly for such impersonation,
a woman on the Volga in the last days of starvation.

57

SYBIL THORNDIKE

I'm in absolute disagreement when you say
I couldn't be a starving woman in a tragic play.
Why not? Why not? If we have the imagination
why shouldn't we portray the suffering of starvation?
We can imagine *anything* if we only would.
'The greatest instrument of moral good,'
that's the imagination, said the poet Shelley.
An actress can play starvation belly or no belly.
If the actress is up to it, starvation won't defeat her.
Imagination is the key.

GILBERT MURRAY

And metre, Sybil, metre!

SHELDON

I guess the so-called acting might get a wee bit closer
if your thespian 's afflicted with *anorexia nervosa*.
It's reality, reality recorded on this reel,
not actors pretending things that they don't feel.

*Sheldon switches off light as if to begin projecting
his film.*

SYBIL THORNDIKE

Honestly! You fucking Yanks!

Sybil switches light back on.

What the fuck
does it matter how I, if I'm acting, fucking look?

GILBERT MURRAY

Sybil, you know that swearing's anathema to me.

SYBIL THORNDIKE

I'm out of your control now. Let me be!

*Sybil Thorndike moves angrily from 'campaign room'
to the table laid for supper. To audience:*

I happen to believe that the theatre permits
an actress to play hunger and still have fleshy tits.
The only thing an actress like me needs to do
is say on stage I'm starving and you'll believe it's true.
She says, 'This is the Volga', she says, 'I'm starving there,'
though she's obese of body and the boards she treads
   quite bare.
The collective imagination of the audience will summon
the freezing snows of Saratov, the starving woman.

SYBIL THORNDIKE

(*as starving Volga Woman*)

Forgive me! Forgive me! I'm so feeble and so weak
from lack of provender I can scarcely even speak.
The last food I was fortunate to feel on my poor tongue
was bread we're forced to make from ground twigs and
   horse-dung.
We give the last hay to the horses then wait till they
   excrete
droppings still studded with nutricious ears of wheat.
A piece of horse-dung bread. And that was days ago.
The insides of our hovels are filling up with snow
since we made them roofless as their thatches, being
   wheat,
were greedily dismantled and ground up for us to eat.
Colder and colder. We'll be brought down to our knees
once river transport's finished when the Volga starts to
   freeze.
Everybody forages. They're desperate. Desperate. So am I.
Without some miracle occuring all of us will die.
Desperate. Desperate for food. It didn't matter what.
Some people, me included, put their pets into the pot.
But couldn't go as far as I saw others do
putting human flesh into their ghastly stew.
Women in labour hope their babies are born dead
and so be spared the burden of more mouths to be fed.

Those who can contrive abortions and the feeble little
   foetus
becomes the grisly broth-base for most desperate corpse-
   eaters.
Some feel the Lord has blessed them if their children die
and their flesh ends up filling for their famished parents'
   pie.
The dead have been dug up. Anything like meat,
even grubbed up from the grave, seems good enough
   to eat.
Burials in any case have to be delayed
because the earth's like iron and frost defeats the spade.
The cold of the region means the corpse is slow to rot
so stays in fresh condition and can end up in the pot.
And for desperate people dying each day of starvation
piles of frozen corpses are a terrible temptation.
They have nothing. The frozen meat's piled high.
Their, our, my stark choice was turn cannibal or die.
So though it was deeply shocking it was no surprise
to see the monstrous mountains diminishing in size
as one by one survivors crept back at night and took
preferably a stranger's corpse by stealth back home to
   cook.
I resisted. I resisted, but in the end had to succumb
and first sucked what bits of flesh were left off a human
   thumb.

I'd seen three babushkas with a steaming cooking pot
and because food was scarce I wanted to know what
they'd managed to scavenge and had to go and look
and find out what they'd gathered that was suitable
   to cook.
From clouds over the cauldron I couldn't really tell
but my mouth began to water simply from the smell.
Through the steam and the shimmer of the cauldron's
   heat

I could see that it was crammed with human hands and
    feet.
Instead of throwing up as you might think I'd do
my mouth watered at the fragrance of their foetid stew.
So many flocked round the cauldron to see if they could
    steal
anything worth gobbling, thumb, big toe, boiled heel.
The crowd around the cauldron couldn't be controlled,
hands were scalded grabbing hands well-casseroled
and my own hand went dipping through the gristly scum
coming up scalded but clutching a cooked thumb.
That first taste was my downfall. Downfall it was not.
I wouldn't have survived this far without corpse-flesh in
    my pot.
I became a cannibal. A cannnibal. The scalded hand
I got from grabbing that first gobbet became a kind of
    brand.
But even if I'm branded no one should exclude
me from humanity because I've lived on human food.
But if you do not wish this disgrace to fall
not just on those who had no choice but on us all,
from the feeble heart beneath this shrivelled breast
I appeal to every one of you, you mothers of the West,
to come to Russia's aid, so that a mother need
not break such terrible taboos when desperate to feed
her children on straw-shreds she's scavenged out of shit
or hellish manflesh *shashlik* sizzling on the spit.
Help me, *pazhalsta*, help me, help my little boy,
we are both almost beyond it. *Spasibo, spasibo bolshoi.*

Sybil Thorndike looks hungrily at laden table.
    She gobbles up food from the plates of the diners
and stuffs it into her mouth, grabbing at anything
edible, creating chaos on the table.
    Nansen, Gilbert Murray, Sheldon, Eglantyne Jebb
and Ruth Fry back off horrified.

Sybil Thorndike sinks behind table, throwing up.
She re-emerges wiping her mouth. Then suddenly
throws up over the table.
Sybil Thorndike shouts angrily at ARA Man.

SYBIL THORNDIKE
Sorry if I'm not *actually* starving.

Calms down. Then breaks the moment with:

I'm starving! I'd enjoy
a little champagne supper across at the Savoy.

Sybil Thorndike sweeps out.
Blackout.

Part Two

Enter the ghost of Hjalmar Johansen with the Greek tragic mask. He is laughing behind it.

GHOST OF HJALMAR JOHANSEN
(*parodying Gilbert Murray*)
And the mouth is always open.
                                     Why? Because
I've cast it as a woman who gives blow jobs to the boss.

He takes the mask and mimes a blow job.

Did you see him flirting? He'll flirt wi' owt, and more
    than flirt,
he'll fuck, will Fridtjof Nansen, almost owt dressed in
    a skirt.
Owt! blonde, brunette, redhead, skinny, squat, fat,
spinsters, widows, wedded, owt 'll do that's got a twat.
The Viking twinkles and the blue-eyed Nordic gaze
were enough to loosen almost any lady's stays.
No better way to get a lady's legs to part
than by being famous for a compassionate heart.
And Fridtjof the hero who 'sends the starving succour'
preys on famine females, the fanny-mad old fucker!
I think this commitment to the so-called caring cause
means wheedling his way into caring ladies' drawers.
As far as cunt 's concerned he thinks Darwin decreed
that Natural Selection needed lakes of Nansen's seed.
His taste's very catholic from chubby 'un to t' skinny 'un,
cunt-hunting justified as 'quintessentially Darwinian'.
I'll be always at your back however much you think
you've finally escaped the one destoyed by demon drink.

Well, I wonder if the demon drink's a lesser demon
than hose-piping the female sex with Fridtjof Nansen
  semen!

Johansen picks up mask again.

Nay, you're no cock-sucker, you're the sort of starving
  mite
them dining do-gooders went on about all night.
It's the open gob of hunger, the eyes that stare,
looking for an angel to sweep down from the air,
but the only angel you'll see with those open eyes
is Death floating out of snow-filled Volga skies.

'ere, poor little bugger, have a bite to eat.
What do you fancy, Murray's veg or Nansen's meat?

Johansen mimes gagging with the mask.

What's that? Speak up. Or do you only speak
Professor Murray's poetic ancient Greek?
What's that?

Johansen bends ear to mouth of mask.

                Can't chew. Can't swallow. Too weak.

*Johansen regards Sybil's pool of vomit. He smells it
to make sure.*

I know! I know! This stuff Sybil spewed up, that'll do.
It's sort of half-digested, good for invalids, this spew.
No. Don't want to? Tell you what. Me first and then you!

*Johansen spoons up some of Sybil's vomit, tastes
some, smacks his lips, then feeds the mask.*

Don't be disgusted. Once you're a ghost you'll spread
even still warm vomit like dripping on your bread.
Ghosts are no longer bound by human inhibition
and break all bounds of behaviour and nutrition.

Johansen takes a knife and a slice of bread and spreads
a good dollop of vomit onto the bread. He takes a
bite out of it.

Ugh? What do you mean: ugh! One day
you too'll guzzle on such gobbets like a ravenous gourmet.
You might throw up at present at the thought of summat
    spewed
being not for mopping up but for slurping up as food.
Be warned: a scoop of cold puke will seem a gourmet
    treat
in the coming days of glacial gloom with nothing left to
    eat.
The future frozen wastes 'll create an appetite
that would even stoop to lapping up a pool of runny shite.
There's human evolution. The triumphant of the species
foraging for nourishment in vomit and in faeces!

Johansen makes to butter another slice. Then puts
down the knife. Looks at the mask.

You'll all look like this poor bugger with his gob agape
gagging for grub in the final sunless famine with no
    escape.
Weigh up your chances. Will the vegetarian croak before
or after the less finickety flesh-wolfing carnivore?
You'll want a cuddle then, to be cradled as you die
without the energy to utter the weakest squeak or cry.

Johansen cradles mask.

When starvation rules the land, why is the food
that famine makes a mountain of, human flesh, tabooed?
They all find cannibalism barbarous. I don't see why.
In extremes like on the Volga you turn cannibal or die.
Only those starvation drove to break the last taboo
had the faintest hope in hell of ever coming through.
Nansen and I should know. We'd both of us be dead

if all we'd done was moan we'd got no wheat for bread.
We were gastronomically inventive out there at the Pole,
creative and not squeamish with all kinds of casserole,
anything, walrus, seal, fox, gull, guillemot,
we shot 'em when we saw 'em and popped 'em in the pot.
A human being's not, thank God, that poor restricted
    brute
the panda of China, only eating bamboo shoot,
and hasn't the survival skills to seek a substitute.
So why be shocked when famine makes men break
taboos formerly binding for survival's sake?
Even those items most tyrannically tabooed
seem in times of famine the most delicious food.
Even the sweetest dearest grandchild but recently defunct
can be the basis of the broth in which horse-dung bread
    gets dunked.
I think this Russian world of such terrible extremes
can hardly be survived on vegetarian regimes.
Poor Professor Gilbert Murray would be quite aghast
that not only meat, but people meat, is part of their
    repast.
Simple meat makes him protest, but he'd protest far
    louder
if he'd smelled the chunks of childflesh cooking in the
    chowder.

Better be a cannibal and live on human meat
than kill the horse you'll need to sow the coming season's
    wheat.
No harvest means more famine, but the question's how,
once they've eaten the horses, will they drag the heavy
    plough?
So full marks to the woman who bakes the undigested bits
that can be carefully salvaged from the droppings a
    horse shits.
I should've asked Dr Murray, Nansen's squeamish chum,

if hay's disqualified as veggie if it's been through a beast's
    bum.
Couldn't it count as veggie-fodder if the half-digested
    straw
has first passed through the bowels of a fellow herbivore?
Those who tried to keep the horses they didn't want to
    slay
used their survivor's instincts and made the precious hay
nourish both horse and owner in a most ingenious way.
The hay 's chewed by the horses. The starving folk can't
    wait
for the horse to digest its dinner and evacuate.
They have to guard the horses, though, in case somebody
    steals
the turds, the starving treasure for their own clandestine
    meals.
A horse fart's a fanfare that alerts shit-thieves to come
and gather the abundance cascaded from its bum.
Unlike Dr Nansen, the Darwinian in me 's fired
to hear of survival practices so poetically inspired.
The Nansen of the North Pole would certainly allow
the cannibal behaviour he seems to balk at now.
The League of Nations' Nansen, in his new soft-hearted
    role,
has silenced the Nansen that I knew at the Pole.
Now that he's embraced this international cause
he's cast aside commitment to old Darwinian laws,
helping bungling Bolsheviks, keeping them alive
when, by the rules of Darwin, there's no chance they'd
    survive.
Nansen of the North Pole, the Nansen that I knew,
would never let a loser jump Selection's fodder queue.
I'm still a Darwinian and for me when those who've died
will appear in public on Nansen's lantern slide
and be projected in the hushed shocked lecture hall

they'll reinforce the maxim that the weak go to the wall.
I bet these starving Bolsheviks felt so blessed in their fate
being visual blackmail for the Western overweight.

Blackout.
As for Nansen's lecture to the various cities in Part
One, screens are flown in until there are three lantern-
slide screens.
Nansen is in front of a lantern-slide screen again.

NANSEN

I came to London twenty-five years ago.
The slides I showed you then were of Arctic ice and snow.
Those years ago I told you that the most uplifting sights
that I had ever witnessed were the Polar Northern Lights.
Now, I fear, it's my duty to put up on this screen
the most horrific pictures I believe you've ever seen.
And I should in fairness warn you that every lantern slide
I'm going to show you will make you horrified.
I who painted the Aurora and its shimmering swathes
  of light
now must show you Russian horrors in bleaker black
  and white.
Once again the landscape is endless ice and snow
but Famine stalks the Volga, laying millions low,
like the poor unfortunates I am about to show.

First slide.
Nansen begins his lecture tour of Britain.

NANSEN
(*before the second screen*)
I came to Newcastle twenty-five years ago.
The slides I showed you then were of Arctic ice and snow.
Now, I fear, I have to put up on the screen
the most horrific pictures I believe you've ever seen.
Famine stalks the Volga, laying millions low,
like the poor unfortunates I am about to show.

68

Second slide.

NANSEN
(before the third screen)

I came to Aberdeen twenty-five years ago.
The slides I showed you then were of Arctic ice and snow.
Now, I fear, I have to put up on the screen
the most horrific pictures I believe you've ever seen.
Famine stalks the Volga, laying millions low,
like the poor unfortunates I am about to show.

Third slide.
Then a sequence of terrifying slides from the
Russian famine appears simultaneously on all three
screens, ending with one of two naked corpses on the
three screens, so that in all there are six.

A brother and a sister on this, my final slide,
to comfort one another held hands as they died.
I leave you this last image to linger in your mind,
two starved siblings, their stiff fingers intertwined.
If all of you here tonight could spare a small donation
we could begin to put a stop to such obscene starvation.

Exit Nansen.
Enter Hjalmar Johansen, looking at the three
screens and the corpses displayed on them.

JOHANSEN

God, you could see that this emaciated bunch
weren't on the guest list at Nansen's 'famine lunch'.
These famine freak-show specimens with shrunken,
    frozen tits
haven't taken light refreshment at the local fucking Ritz.
Did you see them stuff their faces, did you see them
    cramming
cakes into their crumb-flecked gobs to aid the Volga
    famine?

They'd go through the motions of empathetic grief
moued between mouthfuls of tenderly done beef.
Maybe for a moment your fate will make them pause
in mashing more moist morsels in their masticating jaws.

Once you've donned some vestments and been vetted for
    disease
you'd be cordially welcomed to a little wine and cheese.
Best veil your rock-hard titties and your icicle-hung muff,
Aberdeen's a wee bit backward at buffets in the buff.
There'll be lots left for us! If you could escape out of
    the slide
you could wolf the surplus and be richly satisfied.
Be resurrected by your hunger, burst out through the
    screen!
Sink your teeth into the turkey, slurp the soup from the
    tureen.
Don't let it go to waste, eat up, and while you dine
I'll sit down and toast you with what's left of the wine.

Johansen picks up Nansen's pointer.

These corpses are going to make a *corps de ballet* –
if you want to dance the famine, go on, musicians, play.
Get those strings whining, play that pulsing beat
and try to get these corpses to leap up to their feet.
Just get the bloody Bolshoi bowing those violins
and they'll jump up and shake their cash-collecting tins.

Come on, shake a leg, we need to see you rise
and dance Isadora's *Famine* before our very eyes . . .
They don't want their weak hearts torn or their spirits
    rending.
Rise up and dance and show us it's pretending.
You're really only actors who've lost a lot of weight
to portray with more perfection starvation's sorry state.
They must have searched worldwide in the audition
to find such perfect matches for extremest malnutrition.

70

To starved corpses on the screen:

You owe your benefactors a celebratory ballet
to show a spark of gratitude to Hoover's ARA.
Or why not honour, I know, Nansen the explorer
by dancing the joyful ballet the *Aurora,*
composed, played and danced by your lucky Russian kin
who left with Nansen passports the country you're
    stuck in.

A lush musical flourish from the Aurora *ballet.*
    Nothing moves on the slides. Johansen demonstrates
the futility of the exercise.

They'll stay behind the borders of the screen or slide
yearning for a passport to the warmer world outside.

He goads the corpses on the screen.

I know what I'll do. I'll do summat daft
and make these corpses corpse, and once they've laughed
you'll know that they're actors pretending to be dead
and you can worry about what's really real instead.
It won't take much to prove they're just a fake.
When I fart just watch their bony midriffs shake.

He farts. Nothing.

Go on, do some little movement just to show
you're not really dead, like wiggle your big toe.
Go on, you had us fooled. We're mightily impressed
by the thespian corpses. Bravo. Now get dressed.
Each of you have chosen a convincing corpse-like pose
and we applaud your stillness, now put on your clothes.
Move! Make a movement! Let them off the hook.
Show you're alive to them at least and I won't look.

Johansen covers his eyes. Nothing.

Did they move? No? Bad luck, Beaverbrook!

So, you see, they're genuinely dead and nothing's fake
though I wish it all had been for everybody's sake.
I'll leave these to immigrate into your imagination
and escape the confines of photographed starvation.
I'll leave you to try to rouse them, and let you lot try
    to coax
them into dancing, or to corpse at your daft jokes.
Try it all together.

    Johansen begins to go then stops.

                If they're real or just pretend
isn't probably important in the end.

    Exit Johansen, passing on the mask to Nansen.
     A long silence, then a hum begins and grows.
    Then on all three screens simultaneously the corpses
    suddenly sit up and scream.
     The screams develop and re-echo and multiply.
     Nansen and Gilbert Murray listen to the screams
    under the UN logo.

NANSEN

Listen, listen, all these multiplying shrieks
which started at the Volga turn into screaming Greeks.
I thought my spirit, like the *Fram*, could not be sunk
till it multiplied to millions the *Scream* of Edvard Munch.

GILBERT MURRAY

I'm convinced now that Greek tragedy had screams
to show the poetry that followed dealt with great
    extremes.
What irked me as not metrical I know now plays a part
in priming the emotion of the poetic art.
Classicists, myself included, haven't given enough note
to shrieks that are strong enough to scorch the shrieker's
    throat.
When translators give us the inadequate 'Oh woe!'

it's because they didn't know what I now know
that those cries outside the metre the *ai-ai* and the *pheu*
were really intended as an actor's screaming cue,
an occasion outside poetry where the actor could let go,
a scream from the heart that broke the metric flow,
not to be pathetically translated into English as 'Oh woe!'

NANSEN

I rather think that the twentieth-century Muse
has restricted her vocabulary to those *ai-ai*'s and *pheu*s
Sorry to cut you short, Murray, I meant murdered Greeks,
real people and not actors, were uttering those shrieks.
Greeks murdered by the Turks along the Smyrna quays
now in 1922, Professor, not in Euripides.
After so many millennia your Hellenism dies
in Asia Minor with increasing screams and cries.
A migration of this magnitude has not been known
    before
the Greeks were defeated in the Greco-Turkish War.
Already overcrowded vessels, hunger and disease
have killed off 300,000 of the desperate refugees.

I spoke to Johansen in my mind: 'This is one for you,'
I said. 'The Opera House in Athens in 1922!
Like you grinding down my crayons to caulk our kayak
    leaks –
posh opera boxes housing homeless Asia Minor Greeks!
You'd be glad to turn over that velvet plush, to them
not posh perfumed parties applauding *La Bohème*.
Tiers crammed with Greeks made homeless by the Turks
and not come to clap their hands at one of Mozart's
    works.
Each box a curtained flatlet across which washing's hung
instead of those in scent and furs at *Götterdämmerung*.
He'd say: 'Shut up, Dr Murray, homeless people need a
place to eat and sleep and shit, not bloody old *Aida*!'

It's as if this theatre here in London, the Olivier,
instead of being full of people listening to my play,
through some disaster had been compelled to cram
this theatre with refugees, not people watching *Fram*.

NANSEN

Even that, to you, most sacred space of all,
the Theatre of Dionysus, crammed from wall to wall.
Imagine your *Trojan Women* chorus 10,000 times the size
not uttering great poetry but anguished screams and cries.
Murray, I hate to tell you, but you would despair
seeing bivouacs where Hecuba had her premiere.
Bivouacs of rags and branches, an open cooking fire
in the orchestra where Aeschylus first gave his *Oresteia*.
The theatre of Aeschylus, Sophocles, Euripides
now housing hundreds of Asia Minor refugees.
The world's wailing and screaming's going to increase
infinitely greater than the grief of ancient Greece.

*Nansen gets out the marble tragic mask presented to
him by Gilbert Murray and Sybil Thorndike.*

Civilisation as we know it seems destined to collapse
and the tragic masks of Europe will only shut their traps.
Future disasters, future famines, future wars
will slowly close and silence those once always-open jaws.
In the dramas of the future there'll only come
some final means of mourning in a simple sombre hum.
If we can't hope for solutions from our precious League,
what good 's your Greek drama –

*Nansen gives the tragic mask back to Gilbert Murray.
Exit Gilbert Murray, looking at the mask.
Nansen alone.*

                                    – what good my Edvard Grieg?
My spirit longs to fly into the silent sky

untroubled by the screaming the Earth is anguished by.
Above the flight of birds to peer from the Zeppelin
at the wilderness of ice I was my happiest in.
And maybe imagine I see far, far down below
the hut where we wintered buried long ago,
the hut long ago entombed where Johansen and I
learned, despite our difference, to embrace or die.

*Nansen walks thoughtfully to the spot where his
armchair and phonogram were previously placed. He
hears the scratchy Grieg song sung by Eva. It turns into
screams, and from the three phonograms projected on
the shutters comes a 'pure' version of the song towards
which Nansen walks.*

*The projected phonograms change into an endless
Arctic landscape. The Grieg song becomes a huge
orchestral version, enveloping Nansen in his death.*

*A South Bank panorama fades up through the
endless Arctic waste.*

*The NT is reflected in the Thames. The reflection
breaks up.*

*Contemplating the tragic mask, Gilbert Murray waits
outside the National Theatre for Sybil Thorndike,
who enters as if from crossing Waterloo Bridge from
the Savoy. Sybil puts her hands over Gilbert's eyes.*

GILBERT MURRAY
Sybil, is that alcoholic liquor I smell on your breath?

SYBIL THORNDIKE
The champagne was heaven after thirty years of death.
And would you believe it, the Savoy's old *maitre d'*
despite my long absence keeps my table free?
Life! Oysters and champagne at the Savoy!

GILBERT MURRAY
Neither of those items are ones that I'd enjoy!

SYBIL THORNDIKE

Dr Nansen would have bought me some champagne.

GILBERT MURRAY

My hero had some qualities I cannot entertain.

SYBIL THORNDIKE

I just wanted a bit of gladness, life and light
before more oblivion in the Abbey's Arctic night.

Sulky silence.

GILBERT MURRAY

Maybe all my belief in tragedy 's an academic sham.
But I believed in tragedy like Nansen in his *Fram*,
a vessel of the spirit that could withstand the force
of crushing coldness and still move on its course.

What does it amount to, the story that we've told,
the struggle against the ice and men's hearts just as cold?
Not being aware that he was, in fact, a dying man
Nansen published the proposal of his 'AeroArctic' plan
in January 1930. He was going to use
the airship the *Graf Zeppelin* in the first Arctic
    stratocruise.
But by May of the same year my explorer friend was dead,
dying with his North Pole plans still buzzing in his head.
They say that 'AeroArctic' was the last word that he said.
He died on his fjord-side verandah in his chair
whispering 'AeroArctic' and floating through the air
to go the 'farthest north' men can. Neither he nor I
believe there's anywhere to go to when we die
but he sometimes used to say that if there was a soul
and it went anywhere it would be like the Pole.

SYBIL THORNDIKE

The grave's pretty perishing I'd have to agree.
What does anyone amount to? You? Me?

All our performances? Our writings? All for what?
A bright stage, then a blackout without a follow spot.
You and I did our bit for the ailing League of Nations.
The memory of my Hecuba in your great translation 's
the deepest I retain. One of my, I mean *our*, hits.

GILBERT MURRAY

Yes, but its set, those Doric columns, was bombed flat in
    the Blitz.
What after all did our *Trojan Women* do
to help the League to spare us World War Two?
It did as much as it had already done
when it went to America in World War One.
Absolutely nothing! Nothing! It played the USA
when Britain was losing a thousand men a day.
All those what Eliot brands 'Swinburnian' verse
    translations
couldn't hope to save the floundering League of Nations.
Aeschylus trucked out corpses on the ekkyklema.
We've seen the world one corpse-piled ekkyklema,
the corpses of Auschwitz, Dresden, Hiroshima.
A German said, and I'm beginning to agree,
the horrors of Auschwitz silenced poetry.

He looks at the river.

When we reach the Abbey, we'll be separated soon,
let's take a last look at the river shimmering in the moon,
and at the National Theatre. Did you know
Nansen predicts a globe entirely ice and snow?
A world, when the sun cools, a world that will be free
of Evolution's greatest failure, us, Humanity.

SYBIL THORNDIKE

How could I not know? He tried that one on me
as well as all his repertoire of English poetry:
especially, 'Had we but world enough and time,

77

this coyness, my dear Sybil, were no crime.'
I believe his final Ice Age theory may be another ploy
Nansen may make use of when he finds the ladies coy.
Have you yourself acquired one survival skill?

GILBERT MURRAY
Tragedy was my *Fram*. I couldn't hunt or kill.
In Mittagong, New South Wales, as a boy I got the hang
of throwing and recatching the Abo boomerang.

SYBIL THORNDIKE
(*laughs*)
To be truthful I can't begin to picture you,
of all people, Gilbert, boomeranging kangaroo!

GILBERT MURRAY
But just imagine it, the ice!

SYBIL THORNDIKE
Gilbert, I'd rather not.
If I imagine the world's end, I'd prefer it hot.

GILBERT MURRAY
But if Nansen's prediction one day does come true
imagine how it's going to look round here in Waterloo.
Icebergs round the Abbey, maybe Big Ben poking through.
Our Abbey, Parliament, the NT, all below
the everlasting tombstone of Nansen's ice and snow.
A few flags on the tops of buildings might protrude
like that one Nansen planted at his northern latitude.
I fear that my principles won't let me wear furs
as Nansen says we must do when that sad end occurs.

SYBIL THORNDIKE
He offered me a stole of a silver fox he'd shot
and cooked the spine of in his Arctic cooking pot
'I'll offer you,' he said, 'this stole made from my silver fox
to grace your slender neck and shoulders in your opera
   box.

78

Look at its tiny teeth. When you wear it, think of mine
sucking and nibbling the best bits off its spine.'

GILBERT MURRAY

How horrible! How horrible!

SYBIL THORNDIKE

               It was beautiful, the stole.
In exchange he wanted something he was 'starved of at
   the Pole'.

GILBERT MURRAY

Whatever could he mean?

SYBIL THORNDIKE

            I imagine that he means
like you he got frustrated when he couldn't get his greens.

GILBERT MURRAY

So he had a vegetarian streak and I had no idea!

SYBIL THORNDIKE

I suppose he must have pined for sprouts as a Polar
   pioneer!
He had company, of course, but is Johansen who you'd
   choose
to share one's personal passion for the poetic Muse?

GILBERT MURRAY

Nansen and Johansen, even their names rhyme
though they seemed at daggers drawn almost all the time.
They seemed like total opposites, chalk and cheese,
a sort of Arctic Dr Faust and Mephistopheles.

I forgot to ask you, did it please you, the NT?
I'm not entirely certain it's the proper place for me.
No matter how brilliant you are when you translate –

SYBIL THORNDIKE

And you *are* brilliant, Gilbert!

GILBERT MURRAY
                          – all translations date.
I don't for a minute imagine that I dare aspire
to a National Theatre revival of my *Oresteia*.
I'm more than disgruntled to see they only use
bloody Yorkshire roughnecks like Harrison and Hughes.

SYBIL THORNDIKE
In all the years I've known you I've never heard you swear.

GILBERT MURRAY
I'd swear at T. S. Eliot. You know he's with us over there?

SYBIL THORNDIKE
I did, but we haven't spoken.

GILBERT MURRAY
                    Tosser T.S.E.,
with a memorial in the Abbey seventy feet from me!

SYBIL THORNDIKE
How cosy for you both! You must show me where,
and I'll visit. I did a play of his.

GILBERT MURRAY
(*tetchy*)
                          I'm only too aware.
It stuck in my craw and, frankly, it still sticks
that you did Eliot's *Family Reunion* in 1956.
Your betrayal killed me in the May of the next year.

SYBIL THORNDIKE
You were over ninety – don't be tetchy, Gilbert dear.

They enter the Abbey. They hear a hum.

SYBIL THORNDIKE
Whatever's that? Too late to be the choir!

The hum grows louder and more threatening.

GILBERT MURRAY

It sounds like the Furies from the *Oresteia*.

*Gilbert Murray and Sybil Thorndike move through the
Abbey. Gilbert puts the mask back on the monument.
Then in the air and on the ground are the coloured
reflections from the stained glass of the Rose Window.*

SYBIL THORNDIKE

What's that beautiful light, like an Aurora in the air?

GILBERT MURRAY

The moon through the stained glass Aeschylus.

SYBIL THORNDIKE

                              Aeschylus? Up there?
A pagan in the Abbey window. Gilbert, show me where.

GILBERT MURRAY

In the rose's right hand quarter, starting centre, count
one, two, and three is Aeschylus, Greek tragedy's great
    fount.
He's the spirit in my life I most often seem to summon.

SYBIL THORNDIKE

He shares his petal of the rose with the only woman
in the entire circle as far as I can see.
To the right of Aeschylus. Gilbert, who is she?
Who's the woman on his left whose presence seems
    to blaze
through the Abbey in these auroral rays?
It's the red light from her garment that I'm seeing shed
by the moon in the air above me, on my face, my head.

GILBERT MURRAY

You won't believe this, Sybil, it's the Sibyl.

SYBIL THORNDIKE

                              Me?

GILBERT MURRAY

You're the only Sybil who deserves the prefix THE!

SYBIL THORNDIKE

How gallant you are, Gilbert! But she's beautiful, and
   look,
in her left hand, she's clutching her prophetic book.
I wonder if like Fridtjof Nansen the Sibyl can foresee
the freezing of our planet and the end of history.

GILBERT MURRAY

I've been less keen on the Sibyl, and I know you'll
   understand,
since you-know-who used her in his 'poem' *The Waste
   Land*!
And this is Poets' Corner. All those poets who served the
   Muse.
But don't look or stop at that one! It's you-know-who's!

*They start going past Eliot's memorial, and Murray
can't resist stopping.*

GILBERT MURRAY

I lived past ninety years without alcohol or meat
nor ever used language a prof should not repeat.
I want to swear at Eliot but don't want to be
   overheard
by any of the bishops if I use a naughty word.

SYBIL THORNDIKE

Go on, Gilbert, let all that grievance out.
and if you feel the urge to, go ahead and shout.

*Gilbert Murray stamps on T. S. Eliot's memorial and
his shouting creates Abbey echoes.*

GILBERT MURRAY

Eliot, you fucking desiccated cat-exploiting Yank!
It's a pity that you ever left your day job at the bank.
How was that?

SYBIL THORNDIKE
Bravo, Gilbert, that's the spirit, swear!

GILBERT MURRAY
There are so many names I want to call him but don't
dare.

Murray stamps on Eliot's memorial.

SYBIL THORNDIKE
You told me not to stop or look but you just can't resist.
If I didn't know you were teetotal I'd say that you were
pissed.

GILBERT MURRAY
Not, as you say, inebriated but stupidly in thrall
to the kind of petty grievances that sometimes dog us all.
Not . . . intoxicated, no! I'm still steadfastly TT.

SYBIL THORNDIKE
Sadly, as I've noticed, when you're dead you have to be.

GILBERT MURRAY
I promised to take you to see where Larry's laid
then we must part company, dear Sybil, I'm afraid.

*Gilbert Murray and Sybil Thorndike move through
the Abbey and stand over the chiselled plaque under
which the ashes of Laurence Olivier lie.*

SYBIL THORNDIKE
One by one we go. There can't be many left alive.
I was his Jocasta in 1945.

GILBERT MURRAY
(tetchy)
Mmm, the *Oedipus* 'translated' by W. B. Yeats!
Doesn't know a word of Greek yet he still 'translates'!
They all do it now. I doubt if any poets speak
the language they 'translate' from and most certainly not
Greek.

He was Coriolanus. I was Volumnia, his mum.

The continuing hum comes nearer and nearer.

What or who do you suppose it is, that eerie hum?

GILBERT MURRAY

Who's there? Who's there? I thought we were alone.

The hum continues.

Who's there? Are you a ghost that makes that mournful
moan?

*Enter a Kurdish Poet with a sewn mouth. The Poet
wears a placard round his neck that says KURDISH
POET SEEKS UK CORNER. His eyes and ears are also
sewn together.*

Oh God! Who did that to you, poor fellow?

Poet with Sewn Mouth points to self.

GILBERT MURRAY

You?

Well, that's a pretty rum thing for you to do.

To Sybil Thorndike:

How bizarre of the man, indeed how crude, to choose
to come like this, mutilated, to the sanctum of the Muse.
This figure with a sewn-up mouth, this poet, this Kurd,
violates this sacred place where great poets are interred.
With these festering mutilations it seems to me
Poets' Corner is the last place this poor man should be.

Addresses Poet with Sewn Mouth:

Not place! No! Over river! St Thomas's, A&E!

GILBERT MURRAY

Goodbye, Sybil, I'd've written better if I could.

Goodbye, Gilbert! Yes, I know you would.
Wear your laurels, Gilbert.

GILBERT MURRAY
                    I don't think I ought.
I think my poetic efforts have rather fallen short.
I don't deserve them. Besides, I couldn't wear a wreath
that T. S. Eliot's been lying underneath.
I still hear T. S. Eliot –

SYBIL THORNDIKE
                    Oh Gilbert, my poor darling!

GILBERT MURRAY
– stuck in his critic's rictus, superciliously snarling.
On my final exit now all that I'll be hearing
's not audience applause but Eliot still sneering!
My farewell couplet's the very last time
you'll ever hear a terrible Gilbert Murray rhyme.
Farewell, Sybil. Oh woe! I feel a futile failure,
a disgrace to the Muses, to Oxford, to Australia!

> *Gilbert Murray stares at the tragic mask, then smashes
> it, then screams. The screams echo round the Abbey,
> passing overhead above the theatre. Exit Gilbert.*
>   *The Kurdish Poet listens to the echoing scream and
> the hum.*
>   *A red light from the sybil in the Rose Window falls
> on Kurdish Poet.*
>   *Poet with Sewn Mouth hears the hum of a jumbo
> overhead. He listens.*
>   *Sybil Thorndike listens to the hum of the aeroplane
> getting louder and passing overhead above the theatre.*

SYBIL THORNDIKE
And what would you have written if you'd been asked
  to write

a play like poor old Gilbert tried to write tonight?

Sybil moves closer to the Poet.

You're the opposite of Gilbert's mask with sewn up
  mouth and eyes,
but I sense you're seeing something up there in the skies.
Jihadis in the cockpit? Or just a stowaway
trying to enter Britain in a jumbo jet wheelbay?

Plane hum.

Listen! Above the theatre, the hum of a big plane,
from the East or Africa, Conakry, Accra, Bahrain,
following the Thames flight path up to Heathrow,
the river, and the theatres on either side below.
Someone in a window seat wakes up and he can see
down below in London the Thames and the NT.
And maybe, cold and rigid in the dark wheelbay,
about to drop on London, an illegal stowaway.
Listen! Listen! Listen! The great jumbo hum
like the *basso profundo* of some huge harmonium.
If the wheelbay opened now you might look up and see
a corpse crash through the flytower into the NT.
Imagine how it took off, this particular humming plane,
this, let's say, a BA Boeing people boarded in Bahrain.
and the wheels have just retracted in the climbing DC10
and inside the wheelbay with no heat or oxygen,
the stowaway, at that height in the ascending jet,
is fearfully frightened but not quite frozen yet,
a stowaway in total darkness who still dares to think,
as proper cabin passengers are plied with their first drink
and chew their peanuts, still dares to think beneath,
the shivering stowaway with accelerating teeth,
still dares to think (but not for long) that there's a chance
he'll make it to Germany, the Netherlands or France,
or even here to London maybe now tonight,

frozen to death by passage through the Arctic cruising
   height.
This immigrant Icarus who stowed away and flew
was frozen in the wheelbay, and fell on a B&Q.
The thudding thwack of impact headfirst from the sky
on to the concrete car park of a mega-DIY.

   In the voice of a B&Q cashier:

I'm a B&Q cashier. I clocked on at seven am
and passed the splattered brains and briefly glanced
   at them,
only glanced at them, and the feller, then disgustedly
   dismissed
it as some spew-spattered person more than pretty
   pissed.
I think most of us now would make that same
   assumption
that someone had OD'd on their alcohol consumption,
and was sleeping in his vomit. Not the rarest sight
in car parks over Britain after Saturday night.
I just mistook him (OK, I know you think I'm thick)
for one sleeping off his stupor, his face in his own sick.
I did think for a second, they don't go on the piss,
the Pakistanis, and collapse in puke like this.
Then I thought maybe the reason he came to the UK 's
to learn and conform to traditional British ways.
So I didn't notice that the vomit was the poor man's
   brains.

   Sybil Thorndike stops being B&Q cashier.

So many would-be immigrants fall plunging out of planes.
Imagine such migrants falling onto Regent Street
like the raining men in bowlers in that painting of
   Magritte.
Death grants his 'Nansen passports' to every émigré

87

attempting to reach Europe as an airbus stowaway.
The airbus's belly opens, the crowd below it gawps
as a BA jumbo wheelbay gives birth to a stiff corpse.
And the wheelbay opens, the wheelbay opens wide
and disgorges the stowaway frozen stiff inside.
Such frozen corpses tumble out of jumbos in the sky
and thud on to an England they won't be welcomed by.
Dawn's almost here. Now the Sibyl's shed
her red anointing light on this poor poet's head.
With this abandoned laurel wreath this poet must be
     crowned
before sunrise drives me back again into the cold ground.

> *Sybil Thorndike takes a laurel wreath that we saw
> Gilbert Murray try on earlier and places it on the
> Kurdish Poet's head.*
>   *There is the deep hum of a jumbo overhead.*

SYBIL THORNDIKE

Sing the future like the Sibyl. Sing of what's to come.
If it can communicate, your mutilated hum.

> *She makes to leave.*

We, all the Abbey represents. It's had its day.
Wear the laurel wreath. Make poems. Make a play.

> *Sybil Thorndike stands at her memorial.*

And if you do, please, write a part for me.
Nothing too big. Anything. I'm always free.

> *Exit Sybil Thorndike into her memorial.*
>   *The Kurdish Poet becomes flooded with the red
> light from the window.*
>   *The Poet looks up and remains motionless, listening
> to the hum.*
>   *He hums also. His hum is envisioning the end of the
> world.*
>   *Ice appears on the floor of the Abbey.*

At the climax of the Kurdish Poet's aria, the stained glass of the two Rose Windows shatters and falls in pieces on the ice like a broken Aurora.

There is the sound of creaking pack ice.

Icebergs burst through the floor of the Abbey.

Another hum begins, like a great swarm of bluebottles mixed with the aeroplane hum and the hum of the Kurdish Poet.

The humming continues. The Arctic wilderness returns, except that now it is Nansen's predicted future icy end of the world.

There is a totally iced-over Fram.

Into this landscape come two African Boys apparently dressed like Polar explorers, but in fact robed in millions of bluebottles who are making the hum we hear.

Enter Nansen.

NANSEN

You'll see now by the landscape spread in front of you
my prediction, experts have been happy to pooh-pooh,
that the world would end in ice has finally come true.
I had the same disbelief expressed by 'experts' when
    I crossed
Greenland the so-called 'wrong way' and not a man
    was lost,
or when I had the *Fram* built to survive the Arctic ice,
so you'd think that, after scoffing then being proved
    wrong twice,
your contemporaries might have heeded my cooling
    sun advice.
But no! They kept on insisting the opposite was true
till the seas started freezing over and then they knew.

While you are still able to listen and keep warm
the ghost of Fridtjof Nansen has a duty to perform.

These boys have been my inspiration, also my despair,
for their doomed expedition to the Arctic of the air.

To Boys:

For conquering the Aeroarctic in international space
take this flag I used to serve and plant it in this place,
to show, though nobody will see it, that you claim
what you have conquered in no single nation's name.

> *Nansen gives the two African Boys a flag on a stick
> which they plant into the icy stage, It is the UN flag
> with the world in white surrounded by the olive wreath.*

Let it fly, and flap. Though now it won't be seen
there will be ghosts like us remember what the emblems
  mean.
It suits this place. It could have been designed
as the emblem of the iced globe of now doomed
  humankind.
A world past all redemption where no one needs to mark
boundaries round nations all frozen in the dark.
To bring it properly up to date, though, the sea's blue
should also be depicted in icy white-out too,
to reveal the globe's surrender to those superior forces
that keep the orbits going and the planets in their courses,
forces with no hearts or empathy and no scrap of concern
whether in the end our Earth would freeze or burn.

Enter Ghost of Hjalmar Johansen.

NANSEN
Johansen, come here, my friend.

JOHANSEN
　　　　　　　　I know, you told me so.

NANSEN
Hardly time for boasting. I promise not to crow.

JOHANSEN

And yon's the perfect flag to flap at the frozen Pole
of the icy darkness of the snuffed-out hopeful soul.

NANSEN

Did your ashes in their urn like mine identify
with these two young explorers of the Arctic sky?

JOHANSEN

Yes, when I realised they were doomed to die!

NANSEN

The blizzard of my ashes about to blow my bone-urn lid 's
brewing to a fury at the fate of these black kids.
who braved the Aeroarctic of the upper atmosphere
not in bear-fur sleeping bags but flimsy cotton gear.
Explorers, brave ones, with 'no line of retreat',
but with no preparation for what they'd wear or eat.
They were brave explorers but they did not prepare
except for one choc bar they'd clearly planned to share
if they felt peckish once they'd got into the air.
It was found all runny in one boy's rotting hand.
It reset and it remelted as they flew from land to land,
Finally in Africa a sticky choccy glove
rested on the shoulder of the friend he seemed to love.
What they really needed, brave explorers though they
    were,
was a pound of pemmican and a sleeping bag of fur.
They had all of Nansen's bravery with 'no line of retreat'
but didn't prepare like Nansen would for 30,000 ft.
How did they think they could possibly survive
when the Aeroarctic temperature is minus 45?
They entered the Aeroarctic in the sort of cotton gear
worn south of the Equator, where it's very hot all year.
Cotton shirts and shorts, car-tyre flip-flops on their feet –
casual and comfy wear for Guinea's baking heat
but fatally flimsy at 30,000 ft.

In their T-shirts, shorts and flip-flops they didn't prepare
for their pioneering journey to the Arctic of the air.
Just reach Europe, these frozen children thought,
and we'd be warmly welcomed, housed, clothed, taught.
They were frozen, frozen to death, in a DC10 wheelbay,
two adventurous children who naively stowed away.
Think of what could be made of that naive enterprise
and bravery, wasted in that wheelbay in the skies.

The Aeroarctic at the cruising height of jets
gets just as freezing as the North Pole ever gets.
It's as if they'd concentrated all our endless Arctic night
into that dark wheelbay in one seven hour flight.
Those boys didn't have a double bear-fur sack
like we who braved those temperatures and managed to
     get back.
They were a pair of friends, these two desperate refugees,
and a couple can cuddle as the air begins to freeze.
They had to lose their inhibitions, not be shy
of embracing one another to survive the freezing sky.
And they died intertwined, each boy wrapped round his
     friend,
so don't fall from the wheelbay when the wheels descend.
And don't splatter blood on the *Musée des Beaux Arts*
which houses Brueghel's Icarus who also fell as far.
Unlike an AeroArctic Icarus, who freezes and then falls,
their brains aren't aerosolled all over Brussels walls.
No one at *Sabena* knew their bodies were on board.
They left Brussels then flew back. Their bodies froze
     and thawed.
Their embracing corpses at cruising height refroze
and then, landing in hot Conakry, start to decompose.
Freeze/decompose, freeze/decompose on ten successive
     trips
till ground staff in Africa noticed foetid drips
of foul liquid and the dreadful acrid smell

of decomposition from the undercarriage well,
and foul puddles of putrescence on the ground,
and the wheelbay throbbing with a sombre buzzing sound
was probed and prodded and the rotting children found,
in an embrace where each boy seemed to enfold
the other in his arms against the gnawing cold,
the right knee of one between his friend's two thighs.
Like Polar explorers.

Nansen turns to Johansen.

JOHANSEN
Garbed not in furs but flies.
Each one garbed and breeked and hooded by a black
flocking, buzzing, feasting, heaving anorak.
Windblown pelts bespoke from a loud bluebottle swarm
as if they were explorers' furs that kept their corpses
   warm.
That double bag of ours might well have got them through
those regions of sub-zero the *Sabena* airbus flew.

NANSEN
Our bear-fur bag and cuddling might have got them
   through,
As I embraced you, Hjalmar . . .

JOHANSEN
Sir, I cuddled close to you.

NANSEN
We had nothing in common,

JOHANSEN
but we shared our human heat,

NANSEN
and that was what they needed at 30,000 ft.

JOHANSEN
We detested one another,

NANSEN
                    but nonetheless embraced
and survived sub-zero darkness in that Arctic waste.
We shared our warmth despite the hostility we felt,
despite being incompatible,

                    JOHANSEN
                         despite the way we smelt,
If we hadn't cuddled close there's no doubt that we'd've
    died,
but embracing

                    NANSEN
              saved the idealist

                    JOHANSEN
                         and (for a time) the suicide.

                    NANSEN
And might help,

                    JOHANSEN
              for a time,

                    NANSEN
                         when the cooled sun
makes reluctant cuddlers,

                    JOHANSEN
              cuddlers,

                    NANSEN
                         out of everyone.

They put up the Fram *masts and rigging. The iced* Fram
*turns and moves away into the wilderness. The South
Bank, covered entirely in ice, is projected on the back
Olivier shutters. Light fades, leaving the National
Theatre, covered in thick ice, in a spotlight before
blackout.*

The End.